CLASSROOM MINDSCAPES

TEACHING, ENGAGING, AND THRIVING IN HIGHER ED

James M. Lang and Michelle D. Miller, SERIES EDITORS

CLASSROOM MINDSCAPES

An Introduction to Neurodiversity for Educators

SARAH E. SILVERMAN

University of Oklahoma Press : Norman

Classroom Mindscapes: An Introduction to Neurodiversity for Educators is Volume 10 in the Teaching, Engaging, and Thriving in Higher Ed series.

Library of Congress Cataloging-in-Publication Data

ISBN 978-0-8061-9719-7 (hardcover)
ISBN 978-0-8061-9720-3 (paperback)
LCCN 2026001877

The paper in this book meets the guidelines for permanence and durability of the Committee on Production Guidelines for Book Longevity of the Council on Library Resources, Inc. ∞

The manufacturer's authorized representative in the EU for product safety is Mare Nostrum Group B.V., Mauritskade 21D, 1091 GC Amsterdam, The Netherlands, email: gpsr@mare-nostrum.co.uk.

To Elan and Geffie

CONTENTS

ACKNOWLEDGMENTS

As I tell anyone who will listen, I always read the acknowledgments of a book first. I find that it helps me understand the author's perspective, especially when the acknowledgments contain a few personal details that are not part of the main text of the book, so I have attempted to offer that here.

The first people I need to thank are those who literally helped bring this book into existence. It would not exist without Jim Lang's invitation and mentorship. Few corners of the worlds of educational development and college teaching have not been touched by his ideas, and I fondly remember being gifted one of his books in my first-ever teaching job. I sometimes can't believe my luck that I get to be on the receiving end of his advice, which has been another gift. Derek Krissoff and his colleagues at the University of Oklahoma Press also provided support that helped bring this idea from proposal to finished product. Derek made the process of publishing a book with its many stages and periods of waiting feel exciting and even fun, for which I am grateful. Andrew Berzanskis helped shape the title of the book and tolerated my hair-splitting on the various options with good humor. Christopher Stanners found more than a few errors and substantive ways to improve the text and flow of the book, for which I am also very grateful.

I'd like to thank Jennifer Pusateri, Emily Pitts Donahoe, Michael McCreary, Catherine Denial, and Christina Moore, who all provided valuable feedback on the book at critical moments, as well as Tara Mason, Horane Diatta-Holgate, Catherine Clepper,

Caroline Ketchum, Andrew Dell'Antonio, and Cole Denisen, with whom I had important conversations that shaped this work. These conversations occurred in person, on Zoom, and, critically for me, in extended online chats and email correspondence. I offer my thanks to all of them for answering my sometimes unusual questions, and humoring me with discussions about word choices, chapter titles, and more.

This book was further shaped by conversations with colleagues at a number of campuses during the time I was writing it. Of particular importance were discussions with Bill Harder and the faculty at Goucher College, staff and faculty at Davidson College in North Carolina, multiple engagements with Sam Elliot and the faculty at St. Mary's College of Maryland, and faculty and staff at Wabash College. Participants at the Grading Conference in 2025 helped refine some of the ideas about tolerance for error.

I also need to thank the people who have helped shape me, such that I might be the sort of person who could write this book. There is no part of my work in faculty development that is not influenced by Marisella Rodriguez, my first colleague and mentor in the field. Cara Theisen and Kem Saichaie first taught me how to work with instructors at UC Davis, and a day rarely goes by that I don't think about the lessons I learned from them and all the other Teaching Assistant Consultant fellows at UC Davis.

Colleagues and mentors at Goodwin University, especially Diana LaRocco, Robert LeGary Jr., Annjanette Bennar, and Elizabeth Lane, have provided me with many opportunities to teach and facilitate that have helped me become a better educator. They have also provided a model of collegiality and commitment to universal design from which I draw so much inspiration. I wrote a few core chunks of this book while looking out at the Connecticut River from the Center for Teaching Excellence room at Goodwin, a space for which I am very grateful.

I think my family belongs both to the category of "those who shaped me" and "those without whom this book wouldn't exist." My parents, Liz and Jeff Silverman, siblings, Matthew and David

Silverman, and parents-in-law, Sue Gross and Dov Weinstock, have been invaluable sources of support throughout this whole process, and my parents also offered their home for two separate "writing retreats" that helped me bring the project to completion. Moreover, my parents are the people who know best the ways that neurodivergence has been a part of my life since a young age, and who have been an enduring source of support for all that time.

My spouse, Elan Weinstock, and daughter, Geffen Silverman, spent countless hours on the playground, on the tennis court, on the ice rink, visiting friends and family, and generally having adventures together while I was writing this book. This was bittersweet, since I was slightly sad to be hunched in front of my computer but happy to know they were enjoying time together. I am eternally grateful to them for believing in my ability to write this book, cheering me on when I needed it, and most of all for loving me unconditionally. I couldn't have done this without you.

PREFACE

This book, while mostly informational, is also highly personal. The concepts of neurodiversity and neurodivergence explored in these pages have been a deep source of inspiration to me as an educator and faculty developer. But they have also helped me reflect on my own past learning experiences and what role my neurodivergence played in them. I begin this book with a story of how it feels when your cognitive, communication, or relational style is a mismatch with the expectations of a learning situation. While the rest of the book will offer definitions, history, models, and teaching approaches, as well as lots of other stories, I thought it might be good to start with an anecdote about just one neurodivergent student: me.

Overall, I had a rather bumpy start to my graduate program. Every recommendation from my faculty advisors seemed not to work for me. I arrived in the program having identified a research advisor but not a research topic. I was then given the advice that I think nearly every graduate student in an equivalent situation receives: "Go talk to the faculty and other grad students in the department. Learn about their research, ask them questions, and get to know them. This will help you develop your own research idea." I followed this advice to the best of my ability, making appointments with different professors and trying to learn about their work. I also went to other lab groups' meetings. The only problem was that my following these instructions to get to know different researchers did not result in any concrete ideas for my own research project. I was only ever able to develop these based on very detailed consultation of the literature my research advisor suggested and by talking to one of his collaborators. While this is a fairly minor distinction, it was definitely a preview of some larger issues. There seemed to be an assumption that much of the learning and many of the skills I needed to develop as a researcher would appear through a magical process based on *relationships, collaboration,* and *mentorship.* However, every time I tried to initiate these things, I found that they did not further my goals in the way my advisors thought they would. I can't pretend I didn't feel deficient.

During this time, I encountered a major pressure point (which actually turned out to be two): a compulsory oral exam testing general content knowledge of my program's discipline, and a study group that was intended to help students prepare for this test. The study group involved all the first-year students and met one evening a week. It was hard for me to attend for logistic reasons—I didn't live in the town where the university was, and to get home, I relied on a carpool that departed before the study group's meeting time. But the group presented a challenge for other reasons I didn't quite understand myself. It more or less already had an established social order. The other students had met each other at an orientation session that I had missed, and they had already begun spending time together outside work and class. I just couldn't comprehend the flow of the sessions. We always had a specific section of the textbook to review in advance, but then each meeting involved so many tangents and discussions of other topics beyond the exam materials that I struggled to understand the connection between these sessions and the actual exam. The meetings took place during the winter after it was already dark, and I am the textbook definition of a morning person. After a few sessions, I stopped attending. I remember being vaguely aware that I was violating a soft norm of the program ("Attend the exam study group!"), but I couldn't get past my confusion about how this group was supposed to prepare me for the exam. After all, most of the time was spent not studying, or at least studying in ways I knew would not help me in the actual test.

The first time I took that exam, I failed due to genuine confusion about how to prepare for it. I also felt a sense of failure that I hadn't been able to take advantage of the opportunities that the study group purportedly offered. I then had two separate problems to deal with. First, I had neglected to participate in the most important highly social elements of the program: not just the study group but also the weekly departmental seminar and some of the department's various annual parties. Second, I hadn't (yet) acquired or been able to demonstrate the content knowledge that was expected of a doctoral student in the program. I needed to rectify this in my one remaining chance to take that exam.

When I reflect on this experience a decade later, with much greater self-knowledge and a good deal of experience on the instructor side, one thing stands out to me. The faculty in my program assumed that these social experiences would support me in developing the content knowledge and skills I needed. For me, the social expectations made it harder for me to figure out both the content I needed to learn and how to learn it. So much of my mental bandwidth was spent pondering what was "wrong" with me. Why didn't I seem to get anything out of hanging out with the other members of the department? I wondered why I had been so strongly encouraged to work with the other students when the thing that eventually helped me pass all the required exams was so different. I wrote down as many possible questions as I could on index cards with the correct answers on the backs, and practiced recalling the answers until I could reliably do so by heart. I did this alone, in my apartment or in the carpool to campus.

As I do my own teaching and faculty support work now, I look back on this experience and wonder, "What would have helped me have more success in this program?" The routes to success in the program were often framed as "no-brainers"—easy to understand and to follow. To me, some of them didn't seem useful at all, and those I was willing to try presented barriers. As I mentioned, the study group felt difficult to penetrate socially, and was at an inconvenient time. I was not told to register for the weekly departmental seminar as an enrolled student, and thus thought attendance was optional. The department parties regularly occurred on Friday nights and Saturdays, so my observance of the Jewish sabbath precluded attending. When I didn't succeed, some faculty suggested my failure was due to my refusal to take the path they assumed was simple to follow.

I don't offer this story just to show how a program could have been perfectly designed to meet my needs. My ideas here are potentially interesting information for understanding an individual neurodivergent student, but they are only one piece of the puzzle involved in designing inclusive programs. Rather, this story helps to frame this book in human terms. The ways people think, behave, communicate, and learn are variable and complex, and this fact presents many challenges and also many opportunities. As you will read shortly in the introduction, my study of the history of neurodiversity and of the writings of neurodivergent scholars has helped me understand experiences such as this one and provide helpful advice to others. These resources can help us navigate challenges and embrace opportunities, with a greater emphasis on understanding rather than blame.

INTRODUCTION

Before I ever used the term "neurodivergent" to describe myself, I read a book that helped me understand myself, as well as the experiences of many of my students. The book was *Mad at School: Rhetorics of Mental Disability and Academic Life*, by Margaret Price. I first encountered it midway through my graduate program when a colleague and fellow graduate student introduced me to the term "kairotic space," which Price introduces in the book. Based on the rhetorical concept of kairos, or "right time," kairotic space refers to the less formal but still very consequential spaces in academia like office hours, conference breakfasts, and chance elevator meetings where important knowledge is exchanged. As Price explains,

> A classroom discussion is a kairotic space, as is an individual conference with one's professor. Academic conferences are rife with kairotic spaces, including the question-and-answer sessions after panels, impromptu "elevator meetings," and gatherings at restaurants and bars on the periphery of formal conference events. Other examples from students' experiences might include peer-response workshops, study groups, interviews for on-campus jobs, or departmental parties or gatherings to which they are invited.[1]

Price goes on to argue that these kairotic spaces are challenging for people with mental disabilities to navigate.[2] Though these spaces and interactions are "high stakes" (the relationships built and knowledge exchanged are consequential), expectations of them are often hard to discern, and they usually involve live, rapidly unfolding events of a highly social nature. According to Price, when the learning environment is so "kairoticly" structured, students who have difficulty responding, behaving, paying attention, and being physically or mentally present in normative ways will struggle. This was a pattern I had observed countless times among my own students, and I remember talking with colleagues about how to address the potential barriers posed by factors like unstructured office hours and group projects.

I was also struck by how accurately Price's ideas reflected some of my own experiences as a learner, such as those during my first year of graduate school. Price was writing about teachers and students *with disabilities*, which made me wonder what my personal identification with her writing said about me. It seemed clear to me that these kairotic spaces were the ones I had so consistently failed to navigate. So, it was through this exploration of teaching that I first started thinking more seriously about my own "neurodivergence." It was not as if I had never been labeled or diagnosed with one condition or another (I had, several times over). However, having never been diagnosed with a disability that would affect learning per se, I had always minimized my difficulties with school and its highly social or kairotic elements, handwaving around them.

It was revelatory for me to read such a frank and precise description of the kairotic space phenomenon, especially from a fellow college teacher. While I didn't become more public about my neurodivergence until years after this chance encounter with *Mad at School*, reading it at that time opened up a new world for me, in which I did not necessarily have to hide so much of myself.

This book has a simple purpose: to introduce educators to the concept of neurodiversity, its history, and its potential applications in higher education. When you hear or read the word "neurodiversity," you might think of brains, learning, social interactions, and communication styles. And you might think about various disabilities and labels, like autism, attention deficit hyperactivity disorder (ADHD), dyslexia, and Tourette's. While neurodiversity does encompass all these conditions, it also presents an alternative to the idea that these diagnoses are by default and exclusively pathological. At its most basic level, neurodiversity questions the idea of cognitive "normality," that there are objectively "right" ways to think, behave, and learn. Normality happens to have been an important feature of educational systems for a long time. Autistic scholar Peter Smagorinsky notes that schools for teacher training were, until very recently, simply called "normal schools" because of the role they played in setting and enforcing norms among teachers, students, and society at large.[3] When I speak to groups of faculty and staff at colleges and universities, I often start the conversation not by asking what they know about neurodiversity but whether they can identify the norms of their academic disciplines, institutions, or the educational system as a whole. Nearly everyone is able to name a handful of norms, as well as the ways these norms can leave people out of learning experiences. For me, this is the essence of neurodiversity's importance to education—that a more expansive view of how people think, behave, communicate, and learn can benefit everyone in the educational community. That is what I hope to show readers of this book.

Toward a "Neurodiversity Literacy": The Origins and Purpose of This Book

The idea for this book grew out of a series of talks I gave to the general public and at a few colleges and universities. My goal in these talks was to fill a gap in the conversation around neurodiversity in higher education. As more of our students identify as neurodivergent, and some of the challenges that neurodivergent students face during their studies have gained wider recognition, neurodiversity is increasingly understood as an important component of equity and inclusion efforts in higher education. However, few people involved in this conversation have in-depth knowledge of what neurodiversity is, what the origins of the concept are, and the advocacy for neurodivergent inclusion being carried out by what is termed the "neurodiversity movement."

To explain why this book is necessary and how I hope it will help educators, I will draw on scholar Ada Hubrig's concept of "disability literacy," or "the ways we collectively read and understand disability."[4] This concept is not just about knowledge of disability but about understanding the meaning of disability to disabled people, rather than accepting the narratives offered by non-disabled society. As Hubrig writes, "Disability literacy means not just understanding *what* disabled people are saying and organizing for, but understanding the nuances and contexts of *why and how* we say these things." I suggest that educators who wish to do work related to neurodiversity at any scale (whether in the classroom, in student services, or in mentoring and advisory roles) first need to develop what I call "neurodiversity literacy"—that is, an understanding of the important terminology, historical moments and figures, and theoretical concepts of neurodiversity as a social justice movement.

The writings of Margaret Price, the author of *Mad at School* quoted earlier in this introduction, have played a major role in developing my identity and consciousness as a neurodivergent academic. She said of two of her books—*Mad at School* and *Crip Spacetime*—that she wrote them because she couldn't go on *without* writing them.[5] I began writing this book after observing that neurodiversity is a growing area of interest among instructors but that the discussion was not grounded in any in-depth knowledge of the concept of neurodiversity and its history. Like Price, I felt it was hard to go on with some of my neurodiversity work *without* writing a book, as I believe this evolving conversation lacks a foundation of neurodiversity literacy. As an Autistic and neurodivergent person myself, as someone with an interest in the history of neurodiversity, and who has taught about it in my courses, I am relatively well positioned to take on the task of establishing this foundation. To offer one example, as use of terms like "neurodivergent" and "neurotypical" increases, neurodiversity literacy is needed to ensure they are applied accurately.

Neurodiversity is More than (and Not) a Euphemism for Diagnoses and Labels

It is common today in higher education to see the widespread use of the terms "neurodiverse," "neurodivergent," and "neurotypical" without awareness of their histories or particular meanings. Sometimes, "neurodiverse" or "neurodivergent" is used as a euphemism or catchall to cover Autistic students, students with learning disabilities, and students with ADHD. We might wonder: Is it rude to call students Autistic or disabled, or to name the condition for which they need support? What is the difference between neurodiverse and neurodivergent? As I will explain in chapters 1 and 2 of this book, all the terms related to neurodiversity stem from the neurodiversity movement and its goal of opposing the distinction between "normal" and pathological human cognitive functioning. For now, I will offer simple definitions of these terms to set the general context of the book, and provide you with some basic vocabulary. However, it must be noted that these terms have a complex history and are contested enough that a whole chapter on them is warranted. The definitions outlined below are based on those offered by groundbreaking Autistic psychologist Nick Walker in his collection *Neuroqueer Heresies: Notes on the Neurodiversity Paradigm, Autistic Empowerment, and Postnormal Possibilities.*[6]

Neurodiversity first and foremost describes a basic fact about the human population: Cognition varies widely among humans. This reality has been compared to other forms of diversity in humans, such as cultural and linguistic diversity, and more generally to biological diversity, such as the many different species of plants and animals.

Neurotypical refers to people whose style of neurocognitive functioning conforms to societal or cultural expectations.

Neurodivergent can be used to refer to people whose style of neurocognitive functioning does not fall within societal or cultural expectations. Someone who is neurodivergent may have a diagnosis of or identification with autism, ADHD, a learning disability, a mental illness, another condition or a combination of these, but they also may not. As will be explored in chapter 1, "neurotypical" and "neurodivergent" are not biomedical terms, but sociological ones. Accordingly, there is no universal test for whether someone is neurodivergent; that determination depends on societal and cultural norms, and how a person's mind and behavior fit into those.

At this point, as we now have working definitions of these basic terms, it is useful to introduce the **neurodiversity paradigm**. Walker, who first defined this concept, writes that the general term "neurodiversity" is a fact about the world, whereas the neurodiversity paradigm is a political stance. He imagines the neurodiversity paradigm as an alternative to the "pathology paradigm," which is the view that two types of brain exist: one that is "pathological" and one that is "normal." The neurodiversity paradigm instead holds that neurocognitive variation in humans is natural, expected, and positive, and that there isn't a normal brain "any more than there is a normal race, ethnicity, or gender."[7] Based on these ideas, I teach that neurodiversity is not just another way of thinking about autism, ADHD, learning disabilities, intellectual disabilities, and so forth. It is a challenge to the assumption that there even is a "normal" way to think, behave, or learn. The neurodiversity paradigm also notes that the same social power inequalities that affect other types of diversity apply equally to neurodiversity: Powerful or majority groups tend to marginalize or oppress less powerful or minority groups in society. In short, and importantly for educators, neurodivergent people face barriers not inherently or only because of their neurological differences but because of how these differences interact with the norms that society establishes and enforces.

Inclusion Isn't as Simple as a Checklist, Because Neurodivergent People Have Different Needs

It is easy to search Google or ask ChatGPT for "strategies to support neurodivergent students," but the results do not always demonstrate the kind of neurodiversity literacy that I am advocating. Sometimes, results equate "neurodivergence" with autism, even though neurodiversity encompasses a range of experiences and conditions. Advice found this way also tends to assume that neurodivergent students will be registered with their campus disability services office, even though neurodivergent students (not to mention faculty and staff) may not be registered, and may not even have a formal diagnosis at all. Beyond these misunderstandings, the fact that neurodivergence is an umbrella concept encompassing a number of different experiences and conditions means that it is by definition difficult to specify a teaching practice that will be inclusive of the whole group of "neurodivergent students." Some advice for supporting ADHD learners suggests setting a timer during a class activity to help them stay engaged and keep track of how much time they have left. However, this exact practice could make the activity more difficult for students with anxiety or who take more time to process text or visual information. Because of the variable nature of neurodivergence, "access friction"—the phenomenon of multiple access needs coming into conflict—is bound to occur when we attempt to respond to neurodiversity.

Access friction is a useful concept that I will return to throughout the book, because it acknowledges that accessibility and inclusion require negotiation. The manifestations of this friction that emerge with neurodiversity in the classroom are not easily smoothed over. They are often relational matters. In the second half of this book, we will turn our attention to some of these and consider ways to cope with conflicting access needs in the classroom. The issues include but are not limited to the wide range of ways that neurodivergent people relate to disability, diagnosis, and the label "neurodivergent" itself, the relative ease of pointing out exclusionary norms compared with the complexity of addressing them, and the opportunities and caveats of Universal Design. Even if we could wave a magic wand and fix all of the friction around neurodiversity in the classroom, we would likely miss out on some important learning opportunities.

Neurodiversity in Higher Education Includes Students, Faculty, and Staff

A second component of neurodiversity literacy that is needed in higher ed is a broader perspective on who is included in the conversation. I have found that much of the current conversation about neurodiversity on campuses is centered on neurodivergent students. This began with major efforts to support the inclusion of Autistic students and has expanded to other identities and experiences under the "neurodiversity umbrella." This is all positive, but I have noticed that a good deal of the rhetoric around the recognition and support of neurodivergent students suggests that neurodivergence only affects this group. Specialized support programs do exist for students, while there are few or none for faculty and staff. Very recently, there has been an increase in discussion of the experiences of neurodivergent faculty and staff, especially stories of higher ed faculty and staff receiving diagnoses or coming to identify as neurodivergent later in life.[8] A larger picture is coming into focus, in which neurodiversity doesn't relate to a small special-interest group of students but the whole campus community. In this book, I hope to contribute to painting this picture, with examples of and connections between student, staff, and faculty experiences in higher ed. This approach is particularly important to me because I have personally experienced higher education as a neurodivergent student, instructor, and staff member.

"Every Letter of the Alphabet": My Journey with Neurodiversity

Midway through pursuing my PhD in biology (I focused on entomology, the study of insects), I became involved in the teaching and learning center on my campus as a teaching consultant for other graduate instructors, and later as the coordinator of the graduate fellowship program in the center. It was through this center and fellowship that I experienced my first truly supportive academic community, learned about contemporary research into effective teaching methods, and began thinking of teaching and instructional design as potential careers. Excellent mentorship[9] and my gradual loss of interest in my dissertation research led me to decide to pursue educational development after completing my PhD. Since finishing graduate school, I have worked in several teaching and learning centers as a professional development facilitator and instructional designer, and later as a guest speaker.

While working at my first faculty development job, I finally had a bit of time for reflection after the whirlwind of finishing my PhD and moving to another state. I puzzled over some of the diagnoses and labels I'd been offered over the years. I noted that none of them fully described my experiences. This book is not a memoir, but suffice it to say that as a child, I sometimes behaved in ways that confused or concerned my parents and teachers, and had been in and out of various therapies for a decade. I have always been neurodivergent. Although at times I worked very hard to conceal it, I experienced a lot of confusion about other people, social anxiety, and shame about myself. With respect to learning, I was typically classified as a "good student," although I never exactly liked school. My grades were sometimes inconsistent, and in a recent conversation with another neurodivergent colleague, we laughed about having "every letter of the alphabet" on our transcripts. When I look back on my academic experiences, I am certain that the highly social kairotic spaces and other situations with poorly defined expectations contributed to my difficulties. Through reflection and research, and eventually a medical diagnostic process, I came to use the term "Autistic" to describe myself. I have found that this label captures a lot of my personal strengths and challenges, and I use it as a term of identification and pride despite its stigma.

My exploration and greater understanding of my own neurodivergence were also a catalyst for getting involved in a new area of teaching and research: disability studies. Disability studies is a still-emerging interdisciplinary field that examines the nature and meaning of disability in society. I first picked up some disability studies texts to help me with my work in faculty development. I worked with a number of faculty and students with disabilities, and was looking for perspectives that could help me understand why higher education was so hostile to disabled students, faculty, and staff. The books *Mad at School* by Margaret Price and later *Academic Ableism* by Jay Dolmage[10] were constant companions during this time. Out of hunger for more opportunities to engage with the topic of disability, I pursued an advanced graduate program in disability studies, several years after finishing my PhD in biology (after which I thought no one would ever be able to convince me to enroll in an academic program again). When I moved to a new faculty development job, I mentioned my interest and experience in disability studies to a faculty member in women's studies whom I was assisting with an instructional design matter. It turned out that the department was interested in adding disability studies to its course offerings. The process of designing two disability studies courses with Universal Design strategies and then teaching them for the first time (as an openly neurodivergent instructor) was a high point in my academic journey, and it still feels like a privilege to teach these topics.

Teaching in the Neurodiversity Paradigm: A Guide to This Book

These personal and professional experiences have led me to an interest in the neurodiversity paradigm as an important framework for teaching. Recall from earlier in this introduction that the neurodiversity paradigm challenges the idea that there is a right way to think, behave, or communicate. As someone who thinks constantly about the connections between teaching, faculty development, and disability, I have found myself extending this paradigm to teaching and learning: If there is no right way to think, behave or communicate, there can't possibly be one right way to teach or learn. Teaching in the neurodiversity paradigm will require an embrace of neurodiversity and all the opportunities and challenges it presents, rather than adherence to a checklist of practices. I frame teaching in the neurodiversity paradigm as a practice of navigating and negotiating multiple, and sometimes contrasting, needs among students and teachers. Thus, the suggestions I offer for teaching in the neurodiversity paradigm are less best practices and more what Dolmage calls "places to start":[11] questions to ask your students and yourself as an instructor, assumptions to reconsider, and ways of thinking that can help you become more aware of and responsive to neurodiversity in your practice. There is another reason why teaching in the neurodiversity paradigm involves more than some strategies to support neurodivergent students. As it is a set of ideas about the value of cognitive diversity, I believe the neurodiversity paradigm can help instructors think more positively about communication, collaboration, and individual strengths and challenges even when nobody in the classroom (publicly) identifies as neurodivergent. Not all people with cognitive disabilities or differences feel that the term "neurodivergent" describes them well, and indeed, neurodiversity itself is an emerging and sometimes contested concept.

I aim to give readers an introduction to neurodiversity specifically because I hope people working in higher education can develop a better understanding of neurodiversity: what it is and what it isn't. I personally believe the ideas of the neurodiversity movement, and increasingly the scholarship of neurodivergent researchers, include useful lessons for educators that go beyond the (perfectly valid) questions about the limits of the concept of neurodiversity and who is included under definitions of "neurodivergent." These questions are explored in chapters 1 and 2. The concept of teaching in the neurodiversity paradigm is intended to help all instructors who have an interest in neurodiversity, regardless of their own identities or those of their students.

Each chapter of this book introduces an important piece of history or context related to neurodiversity, with the goals of developing readers' neurodiversity literacy and sparking reflection on how the neurodiversity paradigm can (re)shape teaching practice. Because I believe a foundational understanding of the key terms, history, and politics of neurodiversity is important for educators, this book is designed to be read in the order that the chapters are presented.

Chapters 1 and 2 will cover the definitions and histories of key terms and concepts ("neurodiversity," "neurotypical," and "neurodivergent," the neurodiversity and pathology paradigms, and more) as well as the origins of the neurodiversity movement in the Autistic community that developed online in the 1990s. Because these terms have complex histories and variable meanings, educators will benefit from some knowledge of the timeline of the emergence of the neurodiversity concept, key figures and issues, and excerpts from the primary documents of the Autistic rights movement from which the current usage of the term "neurodiversity" emerged.[12] One such document, which provides the title of chapter 2, is the essay "Don't Mourn for Us" by Jim Sinclair.[13] Educators who have ever endeavored to "teach the students you have, not the students you wish you had" may notice some similarities between this principle of acceptance and Sinclair's call for parents of Autistic children to stop grieving the non-Autistic child they never had and build a relationship with the Autistic child they do have. Chapter 2 also details some of the key priorities of the neurodiversity movement and shows how this movement has emphasized the well-being and acceptance of neurodivergent people, despite some internal disagreements. The ideas for teaching in the neurodiversity paradigm in chapters 1 and 2 are supported by examples of how to use our neurodiversity terminology accurately and with respect for their contexts and multiple meanings, and guidelines for critically assessing references to neurodiversity in the educational sphere.

Chapters 3 and 4 cover the relationship between disability and neurodiversity, and the exclusionary nature of much of higher education for neurodivergent students and staff. Chapter 3 provides an overview of how disability and neurodiversity overlap and differ, and how the civil rights of disabled people map on to neurodivergent students, especially in education. As part of this discussion, readers will learn more about the limitations of accommodations, and the different relationships neurodivergent students and staff may have with diagnosis, disclosure, accommodations, or the term "neurodivergent." In keeping with the central principle of teaching in the neurodiversity paradigm—that there is no one right way to teach or learn—I'll discuss the many reasons why students and instructors may choose not to or may not be able to interact with the formal accommodations system, and how we can navigate privacy, disclosure, and inclusion in the classroom. Chapter 4 expands on the opening anecdote in this introduction: Schools have for a long time been institutions that define and enforce "normality." The chapter considers how teachers sometimes uphold the pathology paradigm, and the complexity of responding to exclusionary structures in higher education. Universal Design is the general accessibility framework that served as the inspiration for Universal Design for Learning (UDL), and this history is further detailed in chapter 4.

Chapters 5 and 6 address teaching and learning most directly. Chapter 5 offers a more detailed description of teaching in the neurodiversity paradigm, my framework that integrates neurodiversity history and theory as well as the principles of UDL to acknowledge and embrace neurodiversity in the classroom. I call the transition to teaching in the neurodiversity paradigm a "paradigm shift" to highlight that our response to neurodiversity will involve adopting a whole practice of navigation and negotiation of multiple needs, rather than just completing a simple checklist of practices. Readers will also be introduced to UDL as a potential "ally" framework to neurodiversity, and a place to start in our journey toward neurodiversity-affirming teaching. Chapter 6 explores several "pressure points" relating to neurodiversity in the classroom: group activities, practical activities like labs and simulations, and class discussions. It examines what makes these situations particularly challenging for neurodivergent students to navigate, and how to deal with some of the frictions within them. Throughout the book, I also share ways that teachers interested in supporting neurodiversity can "teach (with) neurodiversity," meaning how they can incorporate ideas, texts, and writers associated with the neurodiversity movement into their curriculum.

There are a number of well-researched, accessible, and up-to-date books on the specific needs of neurodivergent students, such as *College Success for Students on the Autism Spectrum*,[14] *An Educator's Guide to ADHD*,[15] and *Supporting College and University Students with Invisible Disabilities*.[16] I draw from these resources and show how they connect to teaching in the neurodiversity paradigm, with the intention of suggesting strategies for creating shared understanding and empathy when competing needs and access friction inevitably arise.

Although the subtitle of this book indicates that it is for "educators," it is my hope that it will appeal and be useful to people beyond that group, as it provides a concise overview of some of the important terms, historical moments, and figures of the neurodiversity movement. Such knowledge will be helpful to anyone seeking to learn more about neurodiversity. It is also my hope that chapter 4—titled Normal Schools?: The Pathology and Neurodiversity Paradigms in Higher Education—will be of interest to anyone who has participated in higher education as a student, worker, or both, whether or not they are currently educators.

More generally, I hope this book's focus on neurodiversity literacy can provide all readers with the language, context, and confidence to take a neurodiversity perspective in their work and lives. Teaching in the neurodiversity paradigm represents a true paradigm shift, which as Walker writes "requires us to redefine our terms, recalibrate our language, rephrase our questions, reinterpret our data, and completely rethink our basic concepts and approaches."[17] Through this book, I share some of my experiences of how neurodiversity helped me rethink my own identity, my relationships, and many of my teaching practices, and to help you embark on your own journey with neurodiversity.

In service of this goal, *Classroom Mindscapes* is designed to be both informative (it introduces readers to interesting information about neurodiversity) and useful (it contains a host of actionable ideas for educators), but it does not aim to be prescriptive. Every reader is likely to walk away with their own conclusions about how to apply what they learn from this book.

Takeaways and Teaching Invitations

Even though I will share how neurodiversity ideas have shaped my own teaching practice, and ideas for how readers may integrate these ideas into their own pedagogy, I will rarely offer a prescription or advocate for readers to do things just as I do them. My own understanding of neurodiversity is that in our commitment to valuing many different ways of thinking, behaving, and communicating, we should also consider the value of multiple ways of doing things in the classroom. Each chapter of this book ends with a set of takeaways and teaching invitations, which are a summary of the teaching ideas that have been presented in the chapter. The purpose of introducing teaching ideas in the narrative and summarizing them at the end of each chapter is to provide the same information in multiple ways, an idea I draw from Universal Design. When the teaching ideas are presented as part of the narrative of each chapter, I show how they are derived from an engagement with neurodiversity ideas, history, and advocacy. When they are presented in a concise format at the end of each chapter, they provide an action or process that educators can implement knowing that it is derived from this consideration of ideas about neurodiversity and the experiences of neurodivergent people in higher education.

Autistic researcher and neurodiversity movement participant Steven Kapp emphasizes that neurodiversity as a concept has always been about more than differences in the brain[18]—it is also about human relationships, and how we navigate these in a curious and respectful way. To that end, I think of this book as a conversation with readers, using "I," "you," and "we" throughout. As a creature of habit, I'll officially welcome you to this learning experience the same way I begin pretty much every workshop or class that I teach: by saying, truthfully, that I'm excited to learn with you.

1

TERMS AND THEIR HISTORIES

Neurodiversity, Neurotypical, and Neurodivergent

There are many reasons why I began writing this book. A number of them are captured in an advertisement for a teaching professional development workshop that I came across several years ago. (The exact language is slightly paraphrased here.) The title of the workshop was "Supporting Neurodivergent Students: Strategies for Faculty and Staff," which got my attention because of my interest in that very topic. The speakers at the workshop were guests, not members of the community on the campus where the event was taking place, and their primary role was at an autism education center at another university. The event description reads:

> Through this workshop, attendees will learn more about autism spectrum disorder, presenting issues at the college level, and specific strategies to support students in the classroom and beyond. Principles of Universal Design Learning (UDL) will be discussed and implementations of these strategies and design aspects will be presented. Faculty and staff will be actively invited to engage with one another and reflect on experiences working with Autistic students.

Take a moment to read the title and description closely. What do you notice? When I have asked faculty and staff this question, they often say that the title of the event indicates that it deals with supporting "neurodivergent students," but the text of the description only refers to Autistic students. Others have noted that medical and deficit language is used multiple times, with the phrases "autism spectrum disorder" and "presenting issues." Some also note that the description has a positive tone, suggesting that support strategies are available and that it will be beneficial for faculty and staff to reflect on their experience and learn how to apply some of those strategies. All of these are excellent observations—but their variety demonstrates the confusion I sometimes see in how terms are used.

Because language related to neurodiversity is relatively new, and because many of the relevant terms are used in variable ways, it is easy to be confused about how to use the terminology. For example, when I conduct workshops on neurodiversity with faculty, people often ask me if the term "neurodiversity" or "neurodivergent" is the new "politically correct" or preferred way to say "Autistic" or that someone has a learning disability. The thought process behind these comments is well-intentioned and partially correct. Preferred language for matters related to identity, including disability, often will evolve over time in response to social and political developments, and the preferences of the groups in question.[1] Indeed, starting to engage with neurodiversity as educators is a little bit like learning a new language.

In this chapter, we'll explore the history of some of the key terms related to neurodiversity, and their different usages inside and outside higher education. As part of our discussion of the word "neurodivergent," we will examine its general meaning, as well as some of the specific identities, diagnoses, and experiences that could fall under this umbrella term. Even though this book focuses on neurodiversity as an umbrella concept, it is useful to know about a range of the identities and diagnoses it encompasses since these will be relevant to many of the neurodivergent students on our campuses. The chapter focuses on establishing the foundations of our neurodiversity literacy, and how neurodiversity theory can be helpful to us in general as educators.

Neurodiversity literacy, as I define it, is the context-aware knowledge of neurodiversity ideas, and the alternatives they offer to medical-diagnostic perspectives on cognitive differences. This concept of neurodiversity literacy expands on the notion of disability literacy introduced by Ada Hubrig.[2] I want to provide an important caveat here: I don't use the term "literacy" in the exclusionary way it is sometimes used. Jay Dolmage has written throughout his work about how the concept of literacy and tests of literacy have been used for various exclusionary purposes including restricting immigrants from entry into the United States and barring Black Americans from voting.[3] I do not intend the concept of neurodiversity literacy to be a litmus test for who can and can't engage in neurodiversity advocacy work. Rather, I think of it as an affirmative engagement with the roots of neurodiversity ideas. It is also a commitment to linking our discussion of neurodiversity to these ideas: primarily that there is value in neurodiversity and that not all cognitive differences need to be viewed purely as deficits or disorders. Henry Giroux offers the idea of an "emancipatory theory of literacy" in which "literacy is not approached as merely a technical skill to be acquired, but as a necessary foundation for cultural action for freedom."[4] I suggest we build and apply our neurodiversity literacy so we can work toward this freedom, and I hope the information offered in this book can help a broad range of readers engage in action that furthers inclusion.

Most of the terms that are introduced in this chapter, including "neurodiversity," "neurotypical," and "neurodivergent," originated in the discussions and activity of the *neurodiversity movement*. This could be described as a social justice movement with the goal of securing civil rights and full societal inclusion for neurodivergent people.[5] It has significant overlaps with the Autistic rights or self-advocacy movement, which is explored in greater detail in chapter 2. The neurodiversity movement is not centralized, and thus doesn't have official goals. However, all neurodiversity movement activities relate in some way to identifying the drawbacks and harms of pathological or deficit-based approaches to cognitive differences, and involve advocating for autonomy for neurodivergent people. The collection *Autistic Community and the Neurodiversity Movement: Stories from the Frontline*, edited by Steven Kapp, provides an abundance of first-person perspectives from advocates who would consider themselves to be part of the neurodiversity movement, as well as an introduction that sets out the neurodiversity movement's relationship to the Autistic community.[6] This volume is an invaluable resource that I draw on throughout this chapter and chapter 2. It is useful to situate neurodiversity terminology within the neurodiversity movement because this framing can assist with understanding how to use the terms in a sensitive and context-aware way.

Now that we have outlined the basic landscape, let's get into defining our terms and discussing how they can be most appropriately used in an educational context. It is worth noting again that the terms we will discuss are used differently by different people in different contexts. My goal is to provide an accurate overview of where these terms come from and the usages that align with the neurodiversity movement's emphasis on moving away from pathological understandings of cognitive differences. In this way, we can honor the unique origins of these terms in particular neurodiversity movement activities.

Neurodiversity

Neurodiversity can be defined as the cognitive variation in humans, including different ways of thinking, behaving, and communicating. It is probably easiest to think of neurodiversity as a neutral fact about the human population, similar to the fact that humans grow to different heights. While this basic fact is interpreted and applied in a political fashion in the context of neurodiversity movement activities, the term itself does not necessarily have any political meaning. "Neurodiversity" is a compound word (a combination of the prefix "neuro" and the word "diversity," similar to "biological diversity" and "biodiversity"). Where did the word come from? There is some debate and controversy about the term's origins, but one thing that is not disputed is that it originated in the online Autistic community. The term itself is sometimes attributed to Judy Singer, an Australian writer who was active on some of the LISTSERVs and other online communities for Autistic people.[7] One of the most significant lists was called the "independent living LISTSERV" (abbreviated to InLv). It took its name from the independent living movement, which sought opportunities for disabled people to live in integrated settings with non-disabled people, and to exercise autonomy over their own lives. Singer published a book chapter in 1999 which used the phrase "neurological diversity"[8] to refer to the naturally occurring diversity of human minds in reference to the Autistic community's view that autism need not be considered a "disease." While Singer's was the first traditionally published use of the term "neurodiversity,"[9] many people who were involved in the early neurodiversity movement prefer to attribute the term not to one person but to the larger group of mostly Autistic activists who developed the ideas it encompasses. As a group of authors note in a 2024 article on the origins of the concept of neurodiversity, attributing the term to a single person tends to obscure the work that was done primarily on the InLv to develop the concept as we are familiar with it today.[10] They also state that Steve Silberman's best-selling book *Neurotribes: The Legacy of Autism and the Future of Neurodiversity* was significant in introducing the concept of neurodiversity to the wider public.

Even though neurodiversity is in essence a neutral fact, the concept came about in response to pathological understandings of autism. Discussion on the InLv led to the emergence of the term "neurodiversity" because this community was particularly interested in alternative ways for society to view autism, other than as a disease that no one would want. As part of a discussion of how psychologists define autism purely in terms of deficits, Tony Langdon—who regularly posted on InLv—wrote in 1996 that while he did experience some social challenges, he found that he also had notable skills such as those he used in his job in IT. Although he struggled with many everyday activities that other people find easy, the situation was reversed for the technology users he helped at his job: Using the technology was hard for them but intuitive to him. He wrote, "I'm becoming more sure that what allows the human race to progress socially and technologically is the neurological diversity of people. I.e., the atypical among a society provide the different perspectives needed to generate new ideas and advances, whether they be technological, cultural, artistic or otherwise."[11] Likewise, Singer notably compared neurodiversity to biodiversity. To summarize, while neurodiversity is a neutral fact about humans, the term itself is derived from attempts within the Autistic community to describe how Autistic people and others whose cognition differs from societal expectations could bring value to society.

Practical Use

It is useful to think of "neurodiversity" as a noun that describes diversity within a group of people. For example, you might say of a class at a college, "We are looking for strategies to be responsive to the neurodiversity of our incoming freshman class." This would mean that you are interested in engaging with the needs of students with different cognitive styles, including those who are neurodivergent and neurotypical (definitions and histories of these terms are given later in this chapter). The term "neurodiversity" can also refer to the broader set of ideas about the *value* of neurodiversity to society, or the potential benefits of accepting or embracing different ways of thinking, behaving, and communication (see the *Neurodiversity Paradigm* section below). In this usage, an administrator might say, "Our faculty is excited about learning how neurodiversity can inform our teaching and help us become more inclusive educators," indicating that neurodiversity involves an inclusive perspective on cognitive differences. Neurodiversity might also be a useful term to include when discussing other forms of diversity that are important in your classroom, department, office, or institution. For example, an admission officer might say that the institution considers student diversity to be a strength, including racial diversity, gender diversity, religious diversity, and neurodiversity.

Neurotypical

The word "neurotypical" in today's usage tends to mean someone who is not or does not identify as neurodivergent. It is often conflated with the term "normal," which is not a good synonym based on that word's history. Like "neurodiversity" and "neurodivergent," "neurotypical" is a neologism coined by neurodiversity advocates. The history of this term's introduction is recorded by Autistic activist Laura Tisconik in her chapter about Autistics.org, a website where Autistic people gathered to share writing and humor.[12] The genesis of this particular website mirrors the trajectory of much of the autism conversation during the Autistic rights movement—the site was created to be a forum for Autistic adults to share resources and information because most of the existing online resources were geared toward and used by parents of Autistic children. In response to this troubling reality, writers at Autistics.org came up with the idea of creating a spoof website called "the Institute for the Study of the Neurologically Typical." Though clearly identifiable as a satire, the website was meant to mimic actual medical or academic institutes dedicated to the study of autism but replacing autism with the fake diagnosis of "neurotypical syndrome" to refer to non-Autistic people. The point of this satire was to demonstrate how reductive the medical establishment's communication about autism was at the time. The site included FAQs about "neurotypical syndrome," including these selected questions:

> **What Is NT?**
> Neurotypical syndrome is a neurobiological disorder characterized by preoccupation with social concerns, delusions of superiority, and obsession with conformity.
>
> **How common is it?**
> Tragically, as many as 9625 out of every 10,000 individuals may be neurotypical.
>
> **Is there a cure for NT syndrome?**
> There is no known cure for Neurotypical Syndrome. However, many NTs have learned to compensate for their disabilities and interact normally with Autistic persons.
>
> **Could I be NT?**
> Take the Online NT Screening Test.[13]

In his book *Neurotribes: The Legacy of Autism and the Future of Neurodiversity*, Silberman names the term "neurotypical" as one of the enduring contributions of ANI (Autism Network International).[14] It was significant that ANI was the first Autistic-run autism organization, and that its focus was on shifting the conversation away from a crisis narrative about autism and toward greater acceptance of Autistic people and recognition of their unique needs and abilities.

Why is this satirical website important in the history of the meaning of "neurotypical"? Even though the most common usage of this word today is a neutral descriptor for someone whose cognitive style aligns with societal norms or expectations, its roots in Autistic satire of the medical establishment show how unfair and dehumanizing it is to have one's own way of being defined as "disordered" while other people are considered "normal." If you are not Autistic, consider the satirical question "Is there a cure for NT syndrome?" and answer "There is no known cure for Neurotypical syndrome. However, many NTs have learned to compensate for their disabilities and interact normally with Autistic persons." As many neurodiversity advocates have done, Kapp clarifies that this satire and indeed the word "neurotypical" itself are not meant to diminish neurotypical people.[15] Somewhat ironically, at the time the site was taken literally by some readers, who assumed that the authors believed there *was* something wrong with neurotypical people. This is ironic because, as Silberman writes, the prevailing assumption at the time was that Autistic people did not "get" humor at all.[16] There is a significant amount of Autistic humor that aims to shed light on (and, yes, make fun of) the way that society in general thinks and talks about Autistic people. British Autistic comedian Joe Wells has an extended bit about his "non-Autistic brother" in which he details some of his "symptoms": He can't talk unless he is making eye contact; he can't concentrate unless he is in a loud, crowded room; and he is terrible at math. Wells follows this up with the punchline "That's a stereotype, isn't it, that all non-Autistic people are bad at maths? I know some of you can be really good at maths. With the right support, you can achieve anything!"[17] Even though Wells's comedy comes nearly thirty years after the Institute for the Study of the Neurologically Typical, the underlying critique remains the same. Although general impressions of Autistic people have changed for the better, it is still common to hear stereotypes and generalizations that infantilize Autistic people.

Practical Use

The term "neurotypical" can be used to refer to a person or group of people whose cognitive styles align with societal norms. This may mean that they do not have a specific diagnosis of a mental disability. They may not experience friction, or exclusion from most social, learning, and work situations because of their cognitive style. More specifically, neurotypical is a good way to refer to people who are *not* neurodivergent without resorting to the distinction between *normal* and *abnormal*. For example, I once worked with a small college that attracted a large number of Autistic students and students with learning disabilities, as well as many neurotypical students—the campus was about half neurodivergent and half neurotypical by the college's own estimation. We worked together to design a general education course about neurodiversity to help students establish some shared understanding of the idea, and build a foundation for respectful communication and collaboration. If you are neurotypical, using that term to describe yourself could help communicate to neurodivergent people that you understand how your experiences might differ from theirs, as well as the fact that you are an ally.

You may sometimes see or hear the word "neurotypical" being used to denote the opposite of Autistic, ADHD, or another diagnosis. For example, an instructor recently told me about a time when she was helping a lab group that contained a dyslexic student and another student who didn't seem to have any disabilities. She wondered if it would be appropriate to say that pair consisted of "a dyslexic student and a neurotypical student." This is a common usage and could be accurate, but it also may not be. Even if the second student had confirmed that they were not dyslexic, they still might not be neurotypical (they might have another diagnosis or experience that would make them neurodivergent, such as having a mental illness). In such a situation, one good option would be to simply describe the two students using the information you do know: "One student was dyslexic and the other was not. I was helping them to identify some communication methods that would suit both their needs." Another option would be to avoid labeling the second student as neurotypical *or* neurodivergent if you do not have specific knowledge of their neurotype (a term explained later in the chapter). You could say, "I was helping a dyslexic student explain some of her needs to her colleague during a class activity."

Neurodivergent

The adjective "neurodivergent" describes someone whose cognition does not align with societal norms or expectations. It is an umbrella term that covers many different labels and diagnoses, and also includes people without a specific diagnosis whose cognitive style does not match society's norms. The term is a relatively late addition to the vocabulary on neurodiversity. It was first introduced in 2000 by Autistic activist and blogger Kassiane Asasumasu, who went by NeurodivergentK online. She introduced it specifically to expand the conversation about neurodiversity beyond the binary of Autistic and non-Autistic people, to include a broader designation for people who may or may not be Autistic but whose cognitive style markedly differs from established social norms.[18] "Neurodivergent" has subsequently come to include a wide range of diagnoses as well as experiences of cognitive difference that are not described by a diagnosis. The sections that follow outline some of the diagnoses that have become increasingly common in higher education. Before we discuss these diagnoses, it may be useful to take a step back and consider how our interest in neurodiversity and commitment to responding to it does not and should not depend on any specific diagnoses being present, or the disclosure of a disability. Students who are neurodivergent may not have a diagnosis at all, in part because diagnoses are difficult to access and afford, and there are a host of equity issues related to diagnosis. Taking just the example of autism, people of color and women have historically been a lot less likely to be diagnosed with autism, and have often been misdiagnosed with other conditions.[19] I myself, a white woman, was not diagnosed with autism until after I had graduated from my doctoral program, by which time I had received a number of other diagnoses at different points in my childhood and adulthood. From my perspective, I have always been neurodivergent, even though the diagnoses changed; some stuck and some didn't. In addition, students who do have diagnoses may or may not want to disclose them (either the existence of the diagnosis or what specific diagnosis they have). With this in mind, the next sections cover a few common forms of neurodivergence and give some basic definitions. They focus on both strengths and challenges, as well as prevalence in higher education where that information is available. You may notice some common themes as you read these introductions, such as differences in executive functioning that can present challenges in work, educational, and social settings. For other useful summaries of the conditions noted here, the books *Supporting College and University Students with Invisible Disabilities* by Christy Oslund and *The Pocket Guide to Neurodiversity* by Daniel Aherne are excellent resources.

Autism

Autism is a neurodevelopmental profile which, in a medical context, is characterized by social communication difficulties, repetitive behaviors, and restricted interests. A less medical way to describe autism is that it is a difference that affects the way people process information (like sensory information) and communicate.[20] Autism is not a uniform condition, so individual Autistic people have different mixes of strengths and challenges. The general term "Autistic" currently includes people who can participate in daily life, work, and education with minimal support, as well as people who require significant support with such activities. Common challenges that Autistic people report include sensory processing, especially heightened sensory sensitivity and susceptibility to sensory overload, spoken communication, and managing changes in their environment. Autistic people often "stim" or meet their sensory needs by rocking, flapping their arms, fidgeting, or making other movements (in medical language, "repetitive behaviors").

There is a long history of shifts in language preferences to describe Autistic people, so this section can only offer some basic pointers. Most Autistic people prefer to be called "a person/student with autism" or sometimes "with ASD" (autism spectrum disorder), or describe themselves using the adjective "Autistic," with the consensus in the Autistic community seeming to converge on the latter.[21] You may also hear students refer to themselves as "on the autism spectrum" or simply "on the spectrum." When referring to an individual student, it is likely best to just use whatever description they use for themself.

Especially for educators, it is useful to remember that autism is primarily a neurodevelopmental difference, meaning a difference in cognition and perception, rather than an innate lack of certain social or communication skills. While medical definitions of autism often view it as rooted in social deficits, Autistic people's social differences could be viewed as downstream of sensory processing and communication differences.[22] There are abundant stereotypes about autism that color the public's views of Autistic people, and I have noticed that these are also present in higher education. One such stereotype is that Autistic people are either highly skilled in math and engineering, or skilled in those disciplines to the exclusion of others. Some Autistic people do excel in these areas, and they may gravitate toward work with technology because those workplaces are well suited to their style, but many Autistic people also have strong interests and abilities in fields like art, music, and acting. Another stereotype that I have noticed in higher education is the assumption that if someone communicates differently than expected, such as speaking loudly or diverging from expectations about how long to speak for during a group discussion, then they are Autistic. Some Autistic people absolutely do diverge from social communication expectations, but this on its own does not make someone Autistic. Last, to help the faculty that I work with understand some Autistic strengths, I often mention that several Autistic traits are particularly valued in the academic research profession, including attention to detail, intense interests, and self-motivated learning.[23]

ADHD

ADHD stands for attention deficit hyperactivity disorder. While it is also a neurodevelopmental condition, it is characterized by difficulties with attention, impulsivity, and in some cases hyperactivity. A less pathological way to describe ADHD is to say that it indicates differences in a person's attention and concentration. People with ADHD may have difficulty concentrating or paying attention in settings that lack structure or incentives for various tasks, but they may also experience hyperfocus, which is an enhanced ability to focus on one task (often one of particular interest). As with autism, there have been challenges to the idea that ADHD is inherently a disorder, and suggestions that it may be a neutral neurodevelopmental difference that results in challenges when work, learning, and social environments are not accommodating to people with ADHD. In their 2023 book, Edward M. Hallowell and John J. Ratey introduced "variable attention stimulus trait (VAST)" as an alternative name for ADHD, as a neutral rather than pathological framing of this difference.[24] I use the term "ADHD" throughout this book because it is still the one students, staff, and faculty are most likely to be familiar with or use to describe themselves.

ADHD is prevalent in higher education, with up to 12 percent of students reporting traits associated with ADHD, even when rates of diagnosis are lower.[25] The number of students with this diagnosis has also risen over time, whether due to increased enrollment of students who are already diagnosed, or more diagnoses of students during their college years.[26] Unfortunately, ADHD is one of the more stigmatized forms of neurodivergence in higher education, in part because students with the diagnosis often receive accommodations that are themselves stigmatized: extra time on assignments and assessments, note-taking assistance, and permission to record lectures and other class activities. It is not uncommon to see op-eds in higher education media outlets negatively discussing the high rates of ADHD diagnosis and increased numbers of students with ADHD.[27] Fortunately, there are also numerous strong advocates for ADHD learners and employees in higher education including the pseudonymous "ADHD academic," who maintains a website (https://theadhdacademic.weebly.com/) and several social media profiles, and Karen Costa, who authored a book on teaching ADHD learners geared toward higher education.[28]

Challenges for students with ADHD in higher education might include organizational difficulties, like keeping track of the assignments and activities of multiple classes, minimally structured longer-term assignments, or class sessions that provide little structure or punctuation to help maintain these students' focus. Students with ADHD often benefit from clear goals and structure for assignments and class sessions, frequent reminders of upcoming activities or due dates, and a predictable format for class sessions, documents, and course management systems. More positively, people with ADHD may possess strengths including artistic ability, willingness to take risks, and general creative and entrepreneurial interests and abilities.[29]

In addition, there is a growing group of people who are diagnosed (or identify) with both autism and ADHD, often using the hybrid acronym AuDHD.[30] This is an emerging identity, especially because the *Diagnostic and Statistical Manual of Mental Disorders* (DSM) previously indicated that these conditions could not co-occur. Costa offers the metaphor of simultaneously pressing the gas pedal and brake pedal of a car to describe the experience of AuDHD. The gas pedal represents seeking out sensory stimulation, and the brake pedal the management of sensory overwhelm through routine. While a full investigation of the newest research on AuDHD is beyond the scope of this chapter, educators can probably expect the prevalence of this identity to increase among students in the near term.

Learning Disability

The term "learning disability" covers a broad category that includes a number of different diagnoses. It describes the experience of disability in a learning setting, while "learning disorder" is a medical diagnosis with a set of diagnostic criteria and symptoms. Learning disabilities are usually diagnosed in childhood, are lifelong, and can affect how people acquire, process, and retain information. Specific learning disorders (SLDs) include dyslexia, dyscalculia, and dysgraphia—conditions which affect spelling and reading, calculation, and writing or drawing respectively. Dyslexia is the most common learning disability encountered in higher education. Because dyslexic people can have difficulty with fluent reading or spelling, they may experience challenges reading large quantities of printed text or quickly composing written class assignments or emails. Dyslexia is fundamentally a difference in how the brain processes information, so dyslexic people often have particular strengths in other areas including design and spatial reasoning. However, higher education can be very difficult to navigate for students with dyslexia because printed text is so heavily involved in many classes. Writing by hand can also pose a significant challenge for people with dyslexia, and dyslexic students may prefer to type.[31] It is reasonable to expect dyslexic students to need additional time to process information, especially when it is written. Dyslexic students often benefit from repetition of key terms and concepts, as well as the presentation of information in multiple formats. Dyscalculia is a condition that affects numerical processing. While someone with dyscalculia may encounter challenges with calculations, measurement, and other mathematical tasks, they may also demonstrate strengths in creative or strategic thinking. Dysgraphia affects written expression. Someone who has dysgraphia might have difficulty with the act of writing but have particular strengths in other modes of expression.

Dyspraxia

The chances are that you are less familiar with dyspraxia than some of the other forms of neurodivergence in this book. Dyspraxia, also known as Developmental Coordination Disorder, is a neurodevelopmental disability that affects motor planning and coordination. People with dyspraxia can experience challenges with tasks or activities that require a lot of coordination, like driving a car or cooking a multi-step recipe. People who are dyspraxic may be viewed as clumsy if they learn a new skill at a slower pace than other people. Dyspraxic people often demonstrate strengths in more spontaneous activities, like acting or singing, and a number of well-known performers have shared their diagnosis of dyspraxia publicly (the actor Daniel Radcliffe and Florence Welch, the lead singer of Florence + The Machine, are two examples).[32]

Dyspraxic students in higher education may experience similar challenges to other neurodivergent students—with time management, executive functioning, and long-term planning. Dyspraxia also frequently co-occurs with learning disabilities like dyslexia. Specific elements of higher education that could be difficult to navigate for dyspraxic students could be activities that involve a large number of steps or specific movements (e.g., labs).

Tourette's

Tourette's (sometimes called Tourette's syndrome) is a neurological condition that is characterized by noises or movements called tics. It is not a particularly common form of neurodivergence, with less than 1 percent of American adults having the condition.[33] Some people with Tourette's use the descriptor "Tourettic" for themselves, in keeping with identity-first language (there is an explanation of person-first and identity-first language later in this chapter). While Tourette's was not one of the original conditions associated with neurodiversity, an increasing number of people with the condition are interested in considering it to be a form of neurodivergence.[34] Many have called for a rethink of the default assumption that Tourette's causes distress. In addition, a high percentage of people with Tourette's have co-occurring conditions which could include autism, ADHD, learning disabilities, and other forms of neurodivergence. Increasing acceptance of tics and other Tourettic traits combined with the prevalence of co-occurring conditions make a convincing case for including Tourette's among the conditions associated with neurodivergence.

Some challenges people with Tourette's may face in higher education settings are stigma and anxiety resulting from tics, as well as general organizational or executive functioning challenges. Recommendations for teaching students with Tourette's often start with asking instructors to recognize that tics are involuntary and to think about them differently than deliberate behaviors. This requires a significant but vital shift in mindset that will entail balancing different student needs with the knowledge that students with Tourette's will not always be able to control their tics.

Mental Health Conditions

Mental health conditions like anxiety and depression are examples of neurodivergence, though people who have these conditions may not personally identify as neurodivergent. Given neurodiversity's roots in the Autistic rights movements and its later expansion to include other neurodevelopmental conditions like ADHD and learning disabilities, there has been some debate about whether mental health conditions belong in the coalition that has formed around the neurodiversity concept. Because of this perspective, some writers prefer the term "mental disability," which encompasses neurodevelopmental disabilities, mental health conditions, and psychiatric disabilities. Chapter 2 presents an extended discussion of the various perspectives on neurodivergence and mental health conditions.

A Note on Self-Diagnosis

In your role as an educator or in your everyday life, you may encounter people who are "self-diagnosed" with a condition associated with neurodivergence. This is increasingly common, especially with diagnoses of autism and ADHD.[35] Also known as "self-identification," self-diagnosis is a process by which someone determines that they have a certain condition without the involvement of a medical professional. Sometimes, this occurs through interacting with someone who has the diagnosis, or it may happen after the person searches the internet for information on various experiences. Because diagnostic testing can be expensive or hard to access, it is also not unusual for neurodivergent people to be self-diagnosed for the period when they are waiting for testing. Other self-diagnosed people are content to go without a medical diagnosis indefinitely. While having an official medical diagnosis is usually required to access treatments and accommodations at work or school, self-identification may carry its own set of independent benefits. These include increased self-understanding, community with others with the same diagnosis or with neurodivergent people more generally, and a set of resources to draw on to develop coping strategies and self-advocacy skills (you don't need a medical diagnosis to read books and seek out information on the internet).

There are some caveats to self-diagnosis or self-identification. One is that self-identification is not typically accepted as evidence of a disability in a campus disability services office. When working with students who self-diagnose, you may want to clarify the ways you can support them in the classroom without formal documentation. You may need to inform them that if they choose to request accommodations through disability services, they will likely need to seek a diagnosis from a medical provider. Another caveat to self-identification is that individuals genuinely seeking greater understanding of some of their struggles may self-diagnose inaccurately. Writers in the popular media have raised the specific concern that non-professional advice from social media sites like TikTok and Instagram may be overly general and misleading. They recommend that neurodevelopmental conditions such as autism and ADHD are still best confirmed by a medical professional.[36] Those who self-diagnose may be on a journey to a formal diagnosis anyway, so if a student shares their self-diagnosis and expresses an interest in formal diagnosis, you can always guide them to whatever campus or community resources you are aware of that can assist them with this.

Not All Neurodivergent People Have a Diagnosis

Having discussed a number of diagnoses that are associated with neurodivergence, I should mention that not all neurodivergent people have a specific diagnosis at all. If you are wondering how this could be, return to our definition of the word "neurodivergent": someone whose cognitive style diverges significantly from societal expectations. "Neurodivergent" is thus a sociopolitical term rather than a biomedical one. As previously discussed, neurodivergent people may not have a diagnosis because of various economic and other barriers. However, some neurodivergent people may not have a diagnosis because their cognitive style diverges from societal norms in ways that are not captured by available diagnoses. It also bears mentioning that some neurodivergent people may use "neurodivergent" as something of a synthetic term for multiple diagnoses (also known as being "multiply neurodivergent"), so their use of the term may not indicate one particular diagnosis.

A Note on the Adjective "Neurodiverse"

As covered previously in this chapter, "neurodivergent" is likely the original term from within the neurodiversity movement that refers to people whose style of cognitive functioning does not align with societal norms. It can refer to an individual ("Lillian is neurodivergent") or multiple people ("Several students in my organic chemistry class are neurodivergent"). If you have also heard the term "neurodiverse" used in this way, you may be wondering if it is interchangeable with "neurodivergent." I will explain this contested debate and offer my own perspective on it, with the caveat that it is not the only one out there. Some neurodivergent people and their allies absolutely use "neurodiverse" to refer to people with the conditions and experiences often found under the neurodiversity umbrella.

Sonny Jane Wise, a writer and educator on neurodiversity based in Australia, suggests that the most correct usage of the word "neurodiverse" is to describe a group that contains neurodiversity, or a diversity of cognitive profiles.[37] Thus, "neurodiverse" could easily describe any group of people. If you wanted to be more specific, you could say that "neurodiverse" is a descriptor for a group that includes both neurodivergent and neurotypical people. The opposition to describing individuals as neurodiverse, as explained by Wise, is related to the preference for referring to non-white or otherwise minoritized students as "students of color," "racial minorities," or "minoritized" rather than "diverse." Calling individual people "diverse" tends to mark them as the source of diversity, when diversity is really defined by variation within a larger group. For this reason, I use the term "neurodivergent" throughout this book. When I use the term "neurodiversity," it is to refer to the general concept. I use "neurodiverse" as an adjective to describe a group that contains people with different cognitive traits, including both neurodivergent and neurotypical people. However, you will see some people use the term "neurodiverse" as a synonym for "neurodivergent" simply because they prefer it. This is a difference of perspective that I am OK with, even though it is not my own preference.

One question I am often asked is: If neurodiversity is fundamentally a spectrum concept, describing the rich variation in human cognition, why is it necessary to have the terms (and thus distinctions) "neurodivergent" and "neurotypical" at all? Kapp describes the term "neurodivergent" as a term of choice, and a response to stigma. He writes, "While the extension from [the concept of neurodiversity] to group-based identity politics that distinguish between the neurodivergent and neurotypical may at first seem contradictory, the neurodiversity framework draws from reactions to existing stigma- and mistreatment-inducing medical categories imposed on people that they reclaim by negotiating their meaning into an affirmative construct."[38] Neurodiversity—the neutral fact of human beings having cognitive diversity—does not adequately describe the social dynamics that neurodivergent people experience. At least in our current society, people whose cognitive styles differ significantly from expectations can face barriers in their pursuit of social inclusion, educational opportunities, and employment.

Practical Use

The term "neurodivergent" can be used to refer to people whose cognition (as well as behavior or communication) does not align with the norms of a given society or context. In general, a person who identifies as neurodivergent will have some sort of medical diagnosis, or will have diagnosed themself with a particular condition or set of conditions. In the context of higher education, there are three main cases when we might use the term "neurodivergent" to describe a member of the learning community. The first is when a student or staff member discloses a disability that is linked to neurodivergence, such as one of those summarized earlier in this section. Their cognition, communication, or behavior is by definition out of alignment with social norms because they qualify for a diagnosis of a medical disorder. Sometimes when I talk about a coworker with a disability like dyspraxia, I simply call them "my neurodivergent colleague" if what I am saying relates more to the experience of diverging from expectations than to their specific diagnosis. For example, "My neurodivergent colleague and I were commiserating about the difficulties posed by rigorous schedules at academic conferences."

The second case is when a student is noticeably neurodivergent, even if you do not know whether they have a diagnosis. For example, if a student speaks only about one particular area of interest (such as a hobby) during all class discussions, and behaves and communicates in unexpected ways in the context of the norms of higher education, you could plausibly refer to them as being neurodivergent, even without further knowledge.

The third and final case is when students refer to themselves as neurodivergent, which is a situation we may be increasingly likely to encounter. Later in the book, we will further discuss the ways in which the term "neurodivergent" offers a positive sense of identity for those who use it to describe themselves, and some more complex situations in which neurodivergence, disability, and disclosure interact.

The Neurodiversity Paradigm

While the concept of neurodiversity in itself acknowledges the fact of cognitive variation among humans, there is some debate about whether it implies by default an *embrace* of neurodiversity by those who use it. Even though some writers have suggested that the term "neurodiversity" and its use do imply such an embrace of cognitive diversity and a rejection of the default pathologization of cognitive differences, it is helpful to have a term that specifically refers to the embrace of neurodiversity, rather than just acknowledgment of its existence.[39] Nick Walker, an Autistic psychologist, introduced the neurodiversity paradigm as a set of assumptions for viewing the world. It includes the following elements:

1. Neurodiversity—the diversity among minds—is a natural, healthy, and valuable form of human diversity.
2. There is no "normal" or "right" style of human mind, any more than there is one "normal" or "right" ethnicity, gender, or culture.
3. The social dynamics that manifest in regard to neurodiversity are similar to the social dynamics that manifest in regard to other forms of human diversity (e.g., diversity of race, culture, gender, or sexual orientation). These dynamics include the dynamics of social power relations—the dynamics of social inequality, privilege, and oppression—as well as the dynamics by which diversity, when embraced, acts as a source of creative potential within a group or society.[40]

The neurodiversity paradigm thus takes the basic concept of neurodiversity and connects it to social justice. Cognitive diversity is inherently valuable, with no cognitive style being the "right" one, but certain groups still tend to marginalize others in various ways. The paradigm acknowledges this reality, despite its commitment to the inherent value of neurodiversity. The neurodiversity paradigm is an alternative to what Walker calls the "pathology paradigm"—the assumption that there is, indeed, one definable right type of mind, and any minds that differ from this norm can be considered disordered.[41] The pathology paradigm has some parallels with the medical model of disability, which locates disability in individual bodily or mental problems. These parallels are further explored in chapter 3.

Neuroinclusive and Neuronormative

The adjective "neuroinclusive" and the related noun "neuroinclusion" describe an environment or perspective that aims to include neurodivergent people. It was coined even more recently than the terms "neurodiversity," "neurodivergent," and "neurotypical." While the exact origin point and history of the term "neuroinclusive" are not clear, it is enjoying extensive use in some corners of North American higher education. For example, a 2024 guide from the University of South Carolina Upstate for including neurodivergent students is titled "Toward a Neuroinclusive Campus,"[42] and an initiative to support neurodivergent students at the University of Maine is named "Neuroinclusion at UMA."[43]

The term "neuronormative" refers to an environment or perspective that prioritizes what might be considered normal or typical cognitive functioning over any differences from this norm. It could be viewed as the opposite of "neuroinclusive."

Practical Use

You can use the word "neuroinclusive" to mean either "inclusive of neurodivergent people" or "inclusive of both neurodivergent and neurotypical people." The latter usage is not as common since most environments in higher education are designed with neurotypical people in mind anyway. You might say that your department has developed several goals to help it achieve neuroinclusion after some neurodivergent graduate students unexpectedly dropped out of its programs. You could also say of a professional development event, "I thought it was organized in a neuroinclusive way. Each session provided multiple ways to participate, and participants were given ample time to read and process information before they were asked to respond." Perhaps the only potential drawback of using the term "neuroinclusive" is that it is so new that even people who are already familiar with neurodiversity may not know what it means. If it feels like it would be helpful to use the term "neuroinclusive" to describe your own approach or initiatives on your campus, you can always offer a concise definition of what it means. For example, "We are working toward making campus housing a more neuroinclusive environment—one that is inclusive of neurodivergent students. To that end, we are adding sound-dampening materials to walls, and flexibility to lighting and temperature settings in all rooms."

One additional consideration for using the term "neuroinclusive" is that it may be most appropriate in many circumstances to say that your college or organization is *working toward* neuroinclusion rather than that it is *already* neuroinclusive. I sometimes refer to this as a "modest" attitude toward inclusion, or an acknowledgment that inclusion is an evolving goal. As discussed in the introduction, higher education in North America is only in the early stages of responding to the increasing neurodiversity on our campuses, and it is reasonable to suppose that we are at the beginning of a journey with neuroinclusion.

Neurotype

The term "neurotype" denotes a certain type of mind and the traits associated with that type. The most common usage is when people with certain traits or who have a specific diagnosis refer to that collection of traits as their "neurotype." For example, in a meeting a student mentioned to me that she had ADHD and had recently developed some study skills that she felt complemented her neurotype. The term is distinct from "neurodivergence" in that "neurotype" denotes a specific type of mind, collection of traits, or set of differences, while the former refers to the way that a person's cognition differs from societal norms.

Practical Use

It may be useful to use the term "neurotype" if you want to refer to someone's specific set of cognitive traits. You might say that you and a colleague connected over a shared neurotype: dyslexia. You could also say that your student is Autistic, and you are non-Autistic (sometimes called "allistic"): You have different neurotypes.

Applying Your Knowledge of Neurodiversity Language

Educators are probably familiar with the numerous ways we can honor our students' various identities in the classroom. Learning names and pronouncing them correctly, and noting and using students' pronouns are useful examples of how we demonstrate our respect for and sensitivity toward students' identities. Neurodivergent students who do identify themselves to you may refer to themselves in different ways (neurodivergent, disabled, "on the autism spectrum," "I have ADHD," "I am dyslexic," etc.). I recommend noting the language the students and colleagues use about themselves and mirroring it, or simply asking how they like to be referred to.

Person-First and Identity-First Language

In your interactions with neurodivergent students and colleagues, you are likely to encounter both person-first and identity-first language.[44] Person-first language initially emerged as a response to dehumanizing language about disability that emphasized stigma and decreased personhood (e.g., "the disabled"). Thus, many disability advocates and their allies encouraged a transition to referring to "people with disabilities" to emphasize personhood. This model can also be applied to specific disabilities ("person with autism," "people who use wheelchairs"). Identity-first language represented another stage of evolution for the disability movement. As political consciousness grew in the disability community, an alternative perspective on person-first language took hold—that this way of referencing disability made it seem as though disability was secondary to the person.[45] In reality, according to proponents of identity-first language, disability is integral to the person. As disabled academic and writer Katie Rose Guest Pryal notes, the phrase "person with a disability" makes it seem like the disability is something you put in your bag, rather than an important fact about you.[46] Person-first language is common with certain diagnoses ("a student with dyslexia") but not with neurodivergence itself—people rarely say that they "have neurodivergence."

A brief example related to my own identity as an Autistic person: If you are a teacher or a writer, you could consider that most Autistic people don't use medical language to refer to themselves in casual conversation. The two most prevalent terms are "Autistic," and "person with autism," representing identity-first and person-first language respectively. I frequently read books or articles that only refer to Autistic students or even faculty with medical language (such as ASD), rather than using Autistic as an adjective, which is what most Autistic adults prefer.[47] Even if you are working with Autistic people who do not have a strong preference, it may be useful to consider why there is a need to mark autism as a disorder in any particular context, especially if you are aiming for a humanizing and supportive conversation rather than a medicalized one.

Discussing Neurodivergent People in Course Content

The issue of language in teaching and learning contexts remains important even if there are no known neurodivergent people present. For example, instructors in a number of fields may include content about conditions that fall under the umbrella of neurodivergence, the history of those diagnoses, and how different professionals interact with neurodivergent people. It is always a good idea to practice using preferred language in relation to disability and neurodivergence, especially when the texts being studied don't use up to date or preferred language. You don't have to position yourself as an expert on the language, just model appropriate language to the best of your ability. Here are a few examples.

Literature: "The young adult novel The Curious Incident of the Dog in the Night-Time *is well-known for its portrayal of autism.*[48] *During our discussion, we can either refer to the protagonist Christopher as 'Autistic' or 'neurodivergent.' 'Neurodivergent' might be a particularly good term to use if we are discussing the way that other characters perceive Christopher as atypical."*

Textbook: "You'll see in our book that there is a brief mention of 'individuals with neurodiversity.' While it is good that the book tries to bring in the language of neurodiversity, it is usually best to refer to individuals as being 'neurodivergent.' This term means that a person's cognitive traits differ from societal norms."

News media clip: "Today, we will be watching a news clip that includes interviews with several neurodivergent students who are participating in a program on our campus. The program is for students with ADHD and learning disabilities, but we won't know the students' diagnoses when they are interviewed."

Similarly, if you teach in a discipline that frequently uses pathology-based language—such as psychology, medicine, or social work—you may want to include a lesson or two to introduce the language that the neurodiversity movement has offered as an alternative to medical terminology, along with its history. The purpose would not be to invalidate your own field or course content but to provide students with a broader view of the topics they are studying. If you do not feel comfortable enough to discuss neurodiversity yourself, you can always consider inviting a guest speaker or asking a student to do some research and share their findings with the rest of the class. For example, an acquaintance of mine teaches a course on health activism, and I offered some potential sources of information on how various neurodivergent self-advocates had challenged the medical conversation surrounding autism. Students ended up learning about neurodiversity ideas through the health activism lens of their class. Exercises such as these allow you to learn with your students, increasing neurodiversity literacy throughout the whole learning environment.

A Note on the Learning Process, Uncertainty, and Mistakes

As many of us know from our own experiences as learners and teachers, implementing changes in our use of language takes time and practice. If you are new to the vocabulary of neurodiversity, it is reasonable to expect that it will take time to become comfortable using it in everyday conversation. In my view, it is most important to review the terms you want to use, and practice using them on your own or with colleagues. Because of all the stigma associated with disability, we often default to using a euphemism instead of a respectful and accurate term. Here is an example: An instructor comes to me and says, "One of the students in my class is a *different learner.* I need some advice for managing his needs." In a vacuum, this could be a perfectly accurate statement, though it may benefit from additional context and detail. What makes him a different learner, and who is he different from?

If the student has disclosed a particular disability that is associated with neurodivergence (e.g., ADHD), then the statement that he is a "different learner" could be understood as an attempt to avoid discussing his disability. Disabled people have long asked for non-disabled people to avoid calling them "differently abled." Even though this phrase is sometimes intended to be positive (disabled people often have different strengths than non-disabled people), the expression serves to avoid mentioning disability. If a student or colleague does disclose a disability, you can always ask how you can refer to them and describe their disability. For example, I tend to describe myself as "Autistic and neurodivergent," using identity-first language ("an Autistic person"), but you may encounter others who refer to themselves as "on the autism spectrum" or just "on the spectrum."

However, as discussed earlier in this chapter, not all neurodivergent students have a diagnosis or disclose one. Instructors will often ask me, "How should I refer to a learner in my class or a colleague who has not disclosed any particular disability or diagnosis but who I think is neurodivergent?" Here, you have two good options. First, you could just refer to this student as "neurodivergent." This could work well because neurodivergence is specifically not defined by a person's diagnosis but by their cognitive style differing from expectations. You can always clarify the context in which you are using the term "neurodivergent" by saying, for example, "I have a student who is neurodivergent. They haven't disclosed a disability to me, so I am thinking of them as neurodivergent because they have been behaving in ways that I and my students hadn't expected during class." The second option is to skip using the word "neurodivergent" and simply describe their strengths, challenges, needs, behaviors, and communication styles as needed. You might say, "I have a student in my class who often wears sunglasses inside and headphones, and always asks if I can turn off some of the lights in the room. It seems to me like they have some sensory sensitivities." This is the option I recommend, both because it avoids assigning a label to a student who might not use it for themself, and because it offers an opportunity to think more specifically about a student's individual needs and how to respond to them.

Even when you are committed to using the terms "neurodiversity," "neurotypical," and "neurodivergent," you may make mistakes. If you realize you have made a mistake, or someone else notices, your best course of action may be to simply acknowledge the error and correct yourself. If you have anxiety about making mistakes, my advice would be that if using these words is important or useful (and it is to many students, faculty, and staff in higher education) then it is worth building our confidence by using them, rather than refraining from doing so out of discomfort.

Takeaways

This chapter has provided a guide to the language of neurodiversity, some of its history, and how it can be used in our context of higher education. Whether this information was brand-new to you, quite familiar, or somewhere in between, I hope that it provides a useful foundation for our further discussions. As we learned, the final component of the neurodiversity paradigm is that there can be unjust power dynamics with respect to neurodiversity, but also that neurodiversity can be a source of creative potential when embraced. As we will learn in the next chapter, the ideas and language of neurodiversity have their origins in a movement for the acceptance and self-determination of Autistic people. Refer back to this chapter whenever you need a refresher on the terminology around neurodiversity.

Teaching Invitations

- Consider using your developing neurodiversity literacy to review internal or public-facing materials in your educational context (websites, articles, emails).
- Notice if there are any common misunderstandings in your workplace; for example, using "neurodivergent" as a

euphemism for a specific diagnosis, or equating neurodivergence with having a diagnosed disability.

- Consider how you can use the terms introduced in this chapter in your own teaching, even if you aren't using them to talk about neurodivergent students or colleagues. For example, try using them when discussing course content, or characters and media representations.
- Practice using "neurodiversity" and related terminology on your own or with colleagues. This could be a useful way to reduce the perceived stigma around certain terms.

2

"DON'T MOURN FOR US"

The Origins of Neurodiversity in Autistic Activism

In this chapter, we will become acquainted with the community and movement that gave rise to the concept of neurodiversity: the autism rights movement. Sometimes referred to as the "Autistic rights movement" or the "Autistic self-advocacy movement," those involved have sought and continue to seek greater societal acceptance and support for Autistic people. It has also evolved into a broader "neurodiversity movement," and extended its goals to encompass rights and inclusion related to neurodivergence in general. Many of the ideas about inclusion that instructors work with have their basis in social justice notions and movements. Because neurodiversity is such a new concept, few instructors in higher education today will have learned about the neurodiversity movement in high school, college, or even grad school. This is in contrast to ideas about teaching that derive from the civil rights movement, women's movement, LGBTQ movements, and others. While these movements arguably continue to develop in various respects, the neurodiversity movement is undoubtedly still in its infancy. In fact, it only began in earnest in the 1990s.

The term "neurodiversity" was first used in the mid-1990s as part of the online Autistic community's search for a less pathological explanation of differences between Autistic and non-Autistic people. The first Autistic-run autism organization (Autism Network International) was formed in 1992. This was soon after the passage of the Americans with Disabilities Act (ADA) in 1990. The rate of change in the general societal perceptions of autism has been rapid. Readers may be familiar with the unfortunate and persistent myth that childhood vaccines are linked to autism, which has been clearly disproven. However, a useful and somewhat surprising indicator of how far research and public understanding have come even in extremely recent years is that the question of whether vaccines cause autism was salient enough to be discussed on the debate stage between Barack Obama and John McCain in 2008, a mere seventeen years before the time of writing.[1] To say that American society's general attitude toward Autistic people has changed rapidly during this time period is an understatement. There are two important reasons why it is useful for educators to understand more about how Autistic self-advocates and their allies have worked to change public perceptions of autism, and advocated for the rights and acceptance of Autistic people. First, knowing this history will help us understand where the neurodiversity concept came from, and how it has changed over time, which is all part of developing our neurodiversity literacy. Second, I believe the messages of the autism rights movement are useful for educators in their own right. In brief, these are that people must be viewed first as human beings before diagnoses and labels, and that not all differences between people are by default pathological.

This chapter starts by considering why the place of autism in society at the time of the autism rights movement so urgently needed to change. We will discuss medical perspectives on autism, and how neurodiversity advocates have tried to shift the public conversation away from the assumption that autism is fundamentally a disease to one in which autism is a difference that is not necessarily a pathology. As part of this focus, a significant amount of Autistic activism has opposed the idea of a cure for autism.[2] This is based on the idea that autism is what Autistic advocate Jim Sinclair referred to as a "way of being" rather than a disorder.[3] Indeed, research led by Autistics has increasingly suggested that autism is at its root a difference in how people process information. This point distinguishes Autistic advocacy somewhat from the broader disability rights movement, which may advocate for treatments and cures for any number of conditions. *Autistic Community and the Neurodiversity Movement: Stories from the Frontline* is a book edited by Steven Kapp that provides much of the source material for this chapter. In his introduction, Kapp explains that the distinction between Autistic opposition to a cure and the wider disability movement can be represented by one hypothetical person with multiple disabilities. An Autistic woman with epilepsy might desire a cure for epilepsy and not for autism, while still focusing her advocacy on rights, accommodations, and inclusion for both Autistic and epileptic people.

However, opposition to a "cure" as such does not mean that Autistic advocates in the neurodiversity movement do not support any interventions at all for Autistic people—on the contrary! The movement supports the development of Autistic people's skills in communication, learning, social interaction, and daily living. Kapp writes that the neurodiversity movement generally supports therapies and other approaches to supporting Autistic people's functioning, and only "opposes framing these matters in unnecessarily medical or clinical ways."[4] Kapp goes on to make a clear distinction between the outright erasure of a person's autism (whether through medication or behavioral therapies) and the creation of opportunities for them to learn valuable skills and coping mechanisms.

It is this focus on learning rather than curing that resonates with me as an educator. As Kapp writes, "arguably all interventions that have a scientific evidence base for truly helping Autistic people's core functioning involve active learning (by the Autistic person or others), and therefore one might describe them as 'educational'."[5] This idea originally caught my attention because of the phrase "active learning" itself. In my professional context as a faculty developer in higher education, "active learning" is a term used to describe teaching practices that actively engage students in activities or reflections on the material being learned. Kapp uses the phrase slightly differently: His version incorporates growth, personal development, and interpersonal negotiation. Kapp maintains that the types of therapies or interventions that the neurodiversity movement supports will surely involve the Autistic person learning valuable skills. But they will also likely involve non-Autistic family, peers, teachers, and coworkers developing the awareness and skills necessary for working with the Autistic person.

The juxtaposition of the notion of a cure with teaching and learning is one that I believe can be useful for us as educators who teach neurodivergent students, and for those of us who are educators and neurodivergent ourselves. Teaching and learning involve an exchange of knowledge, and that exchange happens in relationships. Educational developer Michael McCreary writes that so often the impulse in teaching and learning is to reach for a cure for an identified problem, when a more realistic response may be to "cope."[6] While coping may feel like an imperfect and imprecise way to deal with any teaching challenge, it could also be described positively as a practice of "noticing, witnessing, acknowledging, experiencing, sharing, enduring, muddling through." This book presents many research-backed ideas for supporting neurodivergent students. Before these, a basic lesson that we can learn from the history of Autistic self-advocacy and the neurodiversity movement is that coping—in the sense of learning, experimenting, listening, and accepting—is often more realistic and more beneficial than searching for the perfect pedagogical "cure."

The Formation of the Autistic Community Leads to Autistic Self-Advocacy

The story of Autistic advocacy, as well as neurodiversity, begins on the internet. You might well argue that pretty much everything interesting that happens nowadays at least partially involves online activity. However, the events and conversations that gave rise to this movement occurred on a very different version of the internet than we experience at the time of writing. Some readers may remember the internet of the 1990s, characterized by email, message boards, slow speeds, and a lot of enthusiasm from early adopters. It was during this period that the Autistic community began to form primarily on LISTSERVs—email groups where one person could email a whole group of others by writing to one address. One significant LISTSERV was InLv, mentioned in chapter 1. It was founded in 1996 by Martijn Dekker, a Dutch Autistic man who had experienced a childhood and young adulthood of isolation and confusion before determining he was Autistic around the time when he founded this email list. In his chapter "From Exclusion to Acceptance: Independent Living on the Autistic Spectrum," Dekker writes about the experience of finding purpose and community for the first time in his life through his management of InLv.[7] He felt that the community flourished specifically because of its text-only medium. He writes, "The text-only email nature of our community, far from being limiting or disabling, was found to be an advantage. We were able to skip all the social rituals and awkwardness and cut right to the chase, undistracted by body language, timing, sensory or eye contact issues, or any of the other autism-related difficulties with socializing." Dekker also reflects on how InLv emerged at a significant inflection point for Autistic people, and catalyzed the development of the concept of neurodiversity. The mix of people on the LISTSERV included those diagnosed in childhood and adulthood, as well as self-identified Autistic people, people who had experienced prior institutionalization, sympathetic family members of Autistic people, and non-Autistic people with other neurological conditions. Judy Singer, who is often credited with first using the term "neurodiversity" in print, was a member and used ideas discussed there in formulating the concept of neurodiversity that became part of her thesis. A 2024 article by multiple neurodivergent researchers, including Dekker, highlights the collective development of the concept by multiple thinkers, including members of InLv.[8] In his history of the LISTSERV, Dekker writes that while it is difficult to pinpoint one single person or post as the origin of neurodiversity as a concept, "What is certain to me is that InLv, due to the ethos of acceptance, inclusivity, and rejection of social and political conformism that I imparted on it, was able to provide the environment in which the idea could emerge."

Some of Dekker's narrative hints at the situation many Autistic people were in prior to the neurodiversity movement: They were largely unconnected with others with the same identity. Dekker recalls that before he began administering InLv, he was relatively isolated and unable to make much contact with other Autistic people. The formation of ANI around this time was significant in that it was the first Autistic-run autism organization. Sinclair, who delivered the speech that became the manifesto Don't Mourn for Us, wrote of an early ANI gathering that "It was an amazing and powerful experience to be able to communicate with someone in my own language. I had sometimes been able to establish meaningful communication with people before, but it always involved my having to learn the other person's language . . . Here, with people who shared my language, meaning flowed freely and easily."[9] While Sinclair is referring to a face-to-face gathering, it is clear that InLv and similar online communities also provided much-needed community-building opportunities which hadn't historically been available.

Don't Mourn for Us

Let's take a look at a key document from this era that went on to be referred to as the first neurodiversity manifesto, demonstrating the connection between ideas in the Autistic community and burgeoning ideas about neurodiversity at that time. The essay actually began as a talk that Sinclair delivered at the International Conference on Autism, but it was later reproduced in full in print. The title, Don't Mourn for Us, references the issue of grief among parents of Autistic children. Sinclair writes:

> Parents often report that learning their child is Autistic was the most traumatic thing that ever happened to them. Non-Autistic people see autism as a great tragedy, and parents experience continuing disappointment and grief at all stages of the child's and family's life cycle. But this grief does not stem from the child's autism in itself. It is grief over the loss of the normal child the parents had hoped and expected to have. Parents' attitudes and expectations, and the discrepancies between what parents expect of children at a particular age and their own child's actual development, cause more stress and anguish than the practical complexities of life with an Autistic person. Some amount of grief is natural as parents adjust to the fact that an event and a relationship they've been looking forward to isn't going to materialize. But this grief over a fantasized normal child needs to be separated from the parents' perceptions of the child they do have: the Autistic child who needs the support of adult caretakers and who can form very meaningful relationships with those caretakers if given the opportunity. Continuing focus on the child's autism as a source of grief is damaging for both the parents and the child, and precludes the development of an accepting and authentic relationship between them. For their own sake and for the sake of their children, I urge parents to make radical changes in their perceptions of what autism means.[10]

Sinclair's first message is that while grief may be a normal response when a parent learns that they have an Autistic child, it is best understood as grief about an unexpected situation and the major adjustments this will bring. Mourning autism itself, Sinclair argues, is not helpful. He has a similar message for autism organizations (primarily those that support parents): The focus of autism organizations should be on understanding how to support Autistic people and their families, rather than providing space for parents to mourn the loss of the typical child they thought they were going to have. Sinclair's second message is that autism is not "an appendage" or "an impenetrable wall," but a "way of being." The reason that the essay is considered by some to be the first neurodiversity manifesto is that it provided one of the earliest arguments in favor of viewing autism as a particular cognitive style that differs from that of the majority: a difference rather than purely a disorder. Under the prevailing assumption that autism is a disease or disorder, many parents believed in and hoped for a cure or at least a treatment that could reveal an imagined person hidden behind the autism. Sinclair counters:

> Autism isn't something a person has, or a "shell" that a person is trapped inside. There's no normal child hidden behind the autism. Autism is a way of being. It is pervasive; it colors every experience, every sensation, perception, thought, emotion, and encounter, every aspect of existence. It is not possible to separate the autism from the person—and if it were possible, the person you'd have left would not be the same person you started with. This is important, so take a moment to consider it: Autism is a way of being. It is not possible to separate the person from the autism.

In summary, Sinclair offers parents the idea that to truly embrace and form an authentic relationship with their child, they will have to accept them as Autistic. At the time, this was a new concept, and Sinclair is careful to balance his paradigm-shifting ideas with a collaborative tone throughout the essay. One of the things I find most powerful and touching about Don't Mourn for Us is that Sinclair does not ask parents to ignore their experience of grief but to consider how best they can address it and protect their children from feeling like an unwanted burden. As an analogy, Sinclair suggests that parenting an Autistic child might feel like bringing up an alien child at first, but the fact that the child needs love and support remains the same as for any other child. At the end of the essay, Sinclair warmly invites parents to "come join us, in strength and determination, in hope and in joy. The adventure of a lifetime is ahead of you."

While the essay addresses the specific audience of parents of Autistic children, its ideas are no less important in education. There are often gaps in experience, assumptions, and expectations between instructors and students that can cause friction and dissatisfaction. As a faculty development professional, I often help instructors think through situations in which they feel that students are arriving in their institutions or individual courses unprepared for the work expected of them. In my experience, this manifests most commonly as a feeling that students are unprepared or unwilling to complete high volumes of weekly reading, or are unable to do certain tasks as independently as expected (e.g., complete a lab activity by following a manual).

Those attempting to help teachers adjust their expectations and teaching methods for the current wide range of students at colleges and universities sometimes advise them to try to "teach the students you have, not the students you wish you had," to paraphrase the title of a 2018 opinion piece in the *Chronicle of Higher Education*.[11] The authors of that piece—educators Sara Goldrick-Rab and Jesse Stommel—highlight the trend in higher education to blame students themselves for perceived changes in student preparedness and engagement over time. Our riposte might be similar to Sinclair's about autism acceptance: It is difficult to form authentic relationships with students while focusing a lot of time and energy on their deficits and how you wish they should be. In the book *Relationship-Rich Education: How Human Relationships Drive Success in College*,[12] authors Peter Felten and Leo M. Lambert describe practices of relationship building that are responsive to students' real lives, rather than any idealized ones. These include high-contact advising, and academic and social support programs, as well as teaching practices like knowing student names as much as possible, and warmly and intentionally referring students to support services instead of giving them a "cold" transfer. Notably, Felten and Lambert discuss how some of the barriers to authentic and rich relationships in education are the result of deficit-based generalizations. Many first-generation students and racially minoritized students experience shame, isolation, and impostor phenomenon throughout their educational journey. While the book does not address disability or neurodiversity explicitly, I noticed that many of the "relationship-rich" educators who are profiled share some of the same values that Sinclair advances in Don't Mourn for Us. Namely, they view students as whole people, inseparable from their cultural, linguistic, and family backgrounds, and understand that there are significant benefits for student success when relationships with real students are prioritized over a focus on the idealized version.

The Ransom Notes Affair: Moving from a Crisis Narrative to an Acceptance Narrative

How does it feel when an innate aspect of how you think and experience the world is compared to a crisis? Many of us with at least one marginalized identity have experienced being part of a crisis narrative (or epidemic narrative), and crisis narratives are as common in higher education as anywhere else. Recall those about students who can't read, write, or even do their own laundry. Autistic advocates have been at the forefront of confronting and dispelling crisis narratives about autism, mostly out of necessity, and have made a major impact. Let's examine one event that emphasizes how recent and how impactful neurodiversity and Autistic advocacy are: the "ransom notes affair."

In 2007, the NYU Child Study Center, which was dedicated to research on childhood psychiatric conditions, began what it described as a public service campaign about various diagnoses, including autism and Asperger's. This consisted of a series of ads in major news and lifestyle publications, each of which was styled as a ransom note written by the diagnosis to the parents of the affected child. Two of these ransom notes were reproduced in an article by Joseph F. Kras, from which I first learned the history of the affair.

> **Autism**
> We have your son.
> We will make sure he will not be able to care for himself or interact socially as long as he lives.
> This is only the beginning.
>
> **Asperger's Syndrome**
> We have your son. We are destroying his ability for social interaction and driving him into a life of complete isolation.
> It's up to you now.[13]

If the copy of these ads makes you recoil, you are in good company: The campaign sparked resistance from Autistic self-advocates and the disability rights community more broadly. One could ask a number of questions about using the metaphor of kidnapping and the perspective on autism it reveals. In the first ransom note, why is it autism that prevents the son from having social relationships or caring for himself, rather than a lack of support, acceptance by his family and other people, and educational and employment opportunities? Why is it assumed that autism will create this barrier for the son's entire life? Similarly, in the second ransom note, why is the condition termed "Asperger's syndrome" the only obstacle to social connection and what consigns the son to "a life of complete isolation?" These ransom notes, and the entire campaign, are based on the pathology paradigm of autism and neurological difference. They also presume that autism is a disease which negatively alters the way a person thinks, behaves, and interacts, rather than an integral component of a person. In his article, Kras points out that the ads made an emotional appeal that dehumanized the hypothetical kids involved. If the purpose of the ads was to raise awareness about conditions that can significantly affect children's health and flourishing, they only succeeded in scaring readers. They offered no information about how to support these children and their families. Kras writes, "Relying on melodramatic stereotypes and caricatures, the ads portrayed children with childhood psychiatric disorders as something they are not: captured, kidnapped, trapped, and incapable of caring for themselves. Such depictions encourage further stereotyping and social isolation and undermine the ability of those depicted in the ads to function autonomously within society." In many ways, it seemed as though the true purpose of the ads was to encourage negative associations with autism rather than to support Autistic people and their families.

Indeed, this was how a number of Autistic adults understood the campaign, and they decided to respond. Primarily led by former president of the Autistic Self Advocacy Network (ASAN) Ari Ne'eman, a petition, letter-writing effort, and public response campaign were organized to provide an alternative to the narrative offered by the Child Study Center. A letter from an anonymous parent of an Autistic child writing under the name "Mom-NOS" read,

> Dear autism,
>
> You don't have my son; I do.
>
> I will make sure that he is never defined by his autism alone, and I will help him to recognize that, although his autism makes some things incredibly challenging, it also brings with it remarkable gifts. I will make sure that we work on challenges. I will make sure that we celebrate his gifts.
>
> This is only the beginning.

After some time, and many response posts, petition signatures, and calls to the Child Study Center, as well as mainstream media coverage, the center made the decision to take down the ads and commit to dialogue with self-advocates before initiating any other public service campaign.

I think there are two important takeaways from the ransom notes affair for us as educators. The first is the importance of treating students and colleagues as people first, even if they have a label, diagnosis, or some other attribute that can be viewed as a deficit. The ransom notes affair reminds us that assumptions about what a diagnosis means—whether they are grounded in fact or not—can lead to fear and blame where there could be a more productive dialogue about establishing understanding and support. I had a conversation recently with an incredibly sincere and well-intentioned college student who was asking me about some of my work around neurodiversity in higher education. He assumed that neurodivergent students who have difficulty with verbal communication are unable to study certain majors that involve seminar-style classes. We discussed the idea that the category of "neurodivergent" contains many different experiences, and the fact that neurodivergent students pursue all kinds of majors, with some students receiving more support and accommodations than others. He told me he came away from our discussion with the realization that he had been making assumptions about certain neurodivergent people he knew personally, based on his own negative associations with their diagnoses.

The second takeaway from the ransom notes affair is the importance of talking with neurodivergent people, not about them. As we will see below, articles or op-eds about "teaching neurodivergent students" or "managing neurodiversity in the classroom" often do not engage with the perspectives of any neurodivergent students or people, or engage only with medical or psychological "experts" like autism researchers or support professionals. The ransom notes campaign and the response to it can provide a lens for considering how neurodivergent students are discussed in popular teaching and learning literature. This includes opinion pieces in news publications, teaching and learning center websites, and popular teaching books. When I am reading these kinds of materials, I like to ask the following questions, which are loosely based on the points made by participants in the ransom notes letter-writing campaign: (1) Does the writing frame the disability as an objective deficit or disorder, or does it explore support and coping strategies that may contribute to success, as well as greater understanding from instructors and peers? (2) Is the writing by a neurodivergent person or does it engage with the perspectives of neurodivergent people? Whether the answer to this question is yes or no, does the writer position themself as an expert on the experience, or do they acknowledge a variety of experiences? (3) Is the (increasing) presence of neurodivergent people treated as a crisis or problem that needs to be solved, a neutral fact, or even an opportunity?

Before we apply these questions to real artifacts, I want to stress that I don't think there are any default wrong answers to these questions. Someone who is neurotypical may be able to provide accurate and useful information about neurodivergent students' experiences based on research and experience. A writer who uses deficit-based language may have done so not because they inherently believe neurodivergence is a bad thing but because they hope to appeal to readers who are more familiar with diagnostic language. The purpose of these questions is to help us apply our growing neurodiversity literacy to the educational conversation around us, and see what perspectives are available and which additional ones it could be useful to seek out. Given this caveat, let's apply this framework to two representative pieces.

The first example is an opinion piece titled "How to Teach Your (Many) Neurodivergent Students" by Katie Rose Guest Pryal, which appeared in the *Chronicle of Higher Education* in March 2023.[14] This article, which I recommend reading in full, takes a humanizing approach to its subjects. It starts with a conversation with an Autistic college student named Emma, which is followed by detailed discussions of some of the types of neurodivergent students who may be in faculty's classrooms and how to support them. Pryal uses "neurodivergent" as an umbrella term to include Autistic students and those with ADHD, anxiety, depression, or another diagnosis. She cautions the reader to avoid stereotypes, noting that for neurodivergent students "the stereotypes about their disabilities do not represent their lived experiences." In the article, Pryal discloses her own neurodivergence, quotes multiple neurodivergent students and instructors, and emphasizes that the experiences of neurodivergent students are quite variable. Throughout the piece, Pryal stresses that neurodivergent students can be successful in college with the appropriate support, and that we should consider ways in which we as instructors can adapt our instructional practices to provide this support. Using the three-part framework I have offered, we could say that Pryal (1) focuses more on support and understanding for neurodivergent students than their deficits, (2) engages with multiple neurodivergent perspectives including her own, and (3) frames supporting neurodivergent students as an opportunity rather than a crisis.

If you are already excited about supporting neurodivergent students, the language and focus of Pryal's piece may seem intuitive. After all, if our ultimate goal is to support and include neurodivergent students, what would be the point of focusing intensively on a deficit-based view of their experiences in higher education? However, this positive approach is a relatively new phenomenon. Compare the article we have just reviewed with one by Libby Sander, also published in the *Chronicle of Higher Education* but a decade earlier, in 2013.[15] In an article titled "Seeking a Deft Touch for Students With Autism-Spectrum Disorders," Sander reports on a talk delivered at the annual meeting of the American College Health Association about the increasing number of Autistic students attending college. Readers are informed that:

> People with autism-spectrum disorders tend to display noticeable differences in their behavior. They might speak loudly, stand very close, and be slow to respond in conversation. They can be extremely sensitive to light and noise, and often exhibit mannerisms like rocking and humming. In college, those compromised social skills can be a significant challenge, Ms. Berkman (the speaker at the conference) said. For people with an autism-spectrum

> disorder, not knowing how to initiate, join, or end a conversation smoothly can be off-putting to others. They also lack a conversational filter, and provide honest, blunt observations at seemingly inappropriate times.

You may immediately be able to spot some of the differences between the 2023 article and this one. The author of this article identifies several differences Autistic students have from non-Autistic people which are not inherently bad (speaking loudly has its place, and rocking and humming aren't harmful by default). These differences are then brought under the umbrella description of "compromised social skills." So, applying our framework, we could say that (1) this piece does seem to equate difference with disorder, and (2) the person quoted was a guest speaker at the conference and not Autistic or neurodivergent themselves (according to the information available). For the third part of the framework, Autistic students are framed as a challenge for professionals who are unfamiliar with their needs but not as a crisis.

It may be a useful exercise to repeat the steps we have taken to analyze these two articles as you review literature about neurodivergent students in higher education, whether that be peer-reviewed journal articles, books such as this one, or "grey" literature such as blog posts, opinion pieces, and university websites. As you develop your neurodiversity literacy, you may be able to identify areas within your sphere of influence where it would be possible to reconsider language that emphasizes deficit and crisis. The opportunities might be small—a flyer your department is preparing to post on a bulletin board or an email going out to a LISTSERV—or larger, such as adjusting the language used on a publicly facing web page at your institution, or suggesting neurodiversity-affirming language to authors in a publication that you edit. In chapter 1, we considered the most-context aware ways to use terms like "neurodiversity," "neurodivergent," and "neurotypical." Here, I hope our discussion of the ransom notes affair shows the paramount importance of choosing words carefully, with attention to neurodivergent people's humanity.

Autistic Participation in the Definition, Diagnosis, and Understanding of Autism

Prior to the emergence of the Autistic self-advocacy and neurodiversity movements, it was solely medical professionals who developed and periodically revised the criteria for autism diagnosis. This changed when the DSM fifth edition (DSM-5) was published in 2013, superseding the previous version from 1994. As discussed earlier in this chapter, the Autistic self-advocacy movement began to emerge online in the late 1990s, so the DSM-5 revisions were the first to be made when an organized Autistic adult community existed.

Kapp and Ne'eman write about their experiences of participating in the DSM-5 revisions as representatives of the ASAN, saying that they used a "combination of social, political, and scientific strategies to 'lobby' the DSM-5 process." This approach was selected because they determined that relationship building was equally important to demonstrating that there was research backing for their recommendations. The ASAN had two notable concerns about the revisions. One was that the criteria for autism diagnoses would be narrowed in certain ways such that people who had previously received a diagnosis (e.g., as children) could be labeled as no longer Autistic on the basis of having developed coping mechanisms that improved their functioning. The ASAN was concerned that if people "lost" their autism diagnosis on these grounds (especially against their will), they might also lose legal protections, support services, and connection to the Autistic community. The other concern was that the criteria might be narrowed in ways that made it harder for women and people of color to receive an autism diagnosis. These groups are thought to be significantly underdiagnosed with autism because of historical biases in diagnostic instruments and among providers themselves.

Kapp and Ne'eman's participation in the revision process yielded some important results. The final language of the DSM entry remained broad, and the criteria for diagnosis were noted to be "illustrative, not exhaustive." This provided more space for people who had historically been left out of diagnosis. Additionally, the final language of the entry acknowledged significant variability among Autistic people and the mix of strengths and challenges that they may experience. To the extent that the DSM shapes the public's perception of autism, this was the first time it had been influenced by Autistic people themselves.

Autistic researchers have shaped other important theoretical and research areas. One involves the question of whether Autistic people fundamentally have a deficit in their social and communication skills. A common framing of Autistic people's communication challenges is that they struggle to understand social cues and to empathize when communicating with non-Autistic people. Autistic researcher Damian Milton views this framing as unnecessarily one-sided and proposes an alternative explanation for these challenges called the "double empathy problem."[16] Even if it is true that Autistic people struggle to communicate and empathize with non-Autistic people, the reverse is also true: Non-Autistic people struggle to communicate or empathize with Autistic people, and often don't feel obligated to try. This new perspective reframes communication differences that involve neurodivergence as relational issues, rather than ones of essential deficit.

Kapp has also critiqued the way that assuming Autistic people have deficient social skills introduces bias into research.[17] One idea he raises is that when a difference such as autism is defined exclusively as a deficit, then even neutral traits tend to be interpreted through the lens of deficit. He refers to a study where researchers looked at differences between Autistic and non-Autistic participants' laughter, with a particular focus on unvoiced laughter—less genuine laughter that is usually not accompanied by voiced sound. The researchers argued that unvoiced laughter is used to negotiate social interactions rather than reflect a person's internal state of being amused (e.g., the laugh you use to indicate you know a joke is being told, rather than because you think the joke is funny).[18] The results showed that Autistic participants engaged in less unvoiced laughter than the non-Autistic participants. The researchers interpreted this difference as a deficit in the Autistic participants, even while admitting that the laughter they did engage in was "affectively engaging" to other people. Kapp explains that this is an example of confirmation bias. When I read the conclusion of the paper, I agreed, because the authors specifically rejected a potentially neutral interpretation of the results in favor of the pre-established principle that Autistic people are characterized by social deficits. I feel that this hazard is present in the classroom as well: We can fall into the trap of assuming a student has poor social skills or poor comprehension skills, and using that lens to interpret every difference from expectations.

Autistic researchers and self-advocates have maintained an interest in the debate about whether it is appropriate to describe Autistic people as "severely Autistic" or to use functioning labels such as "high functioning" or "low functioning." The two main concerns with these categories are that Autistic people can have unique combinations of strengths and challenges that are not well described in terms of "high" or "low" functioning, and that it is generally more respectful to characterize people by the support they need, rather than how well or poorly they function.[19]

These conversations connect to much larger histories of autism diagnosis and the impact of language on how we understand neurodiversity. In an interview, Autistic researcher Michelle Dawson discusses her feeling that there is no evidence-based definition of "severity" in the autism conversation, and that much of the discussion of severity conflates an Autistic person's co-occurring disabilities with autism itself.[20] For example, an Autistic person may have a seizure disorder that causes significant impairment. For Dawson, referring to an Autistic person who has several disabilities that make them significantly different from a typical person as "severely Autistic" is a bit like looking at a person who has a broken leg and a sprained ankle and saying that they have a severely broken leg. In this analogy, the different injuries and how they may be related or distinct is glossed over. The sprained ankle may be from a completely different accident, or it may be related to the broken leg. Undoubtedly, having both of these conditions presents more challenges for mobility and other pursuits than just having one of them, but information is lost when they are both understood as part of the broken leg. Dawson also critiques the concept of severity as equating difference with inferiority. In response to a question about how atypical abilities are often underrated, she says,

> It seems to be something that people are very bad at, to detect abilities and worth in highly atypical individuals. For sure, you see this very much in autism with the whole notion of severity, and this is not defined. There is no workable definition of autism severity. People use that word all the time. They use it to mean that somebody's had a bad outcome, or that someone is badly behaved, or that somebody performs badly on an IQ test, and so on. There is something bad going on here, and it's sort of the equation that the more atypical a person is, the worse they must be. They must not be intelligent. There must be something extra wrong, more wrong about their behavior, and so on. Now, this is where I'm very familiar with the whole history of this, and it's obviously problematic. We don't—I *hope* we don't look at a blind person who is a successful lawyer and assume that he is only very mildly blind or barely blind at all, and then look at a blind person who has a very bad outcome and assume that they must be very severely blind. We do make those kinds of judgments in autism, saying, "The more atypical the person is, the worse they must be in some sense."

This conversation may be relevant to educators directly and indirectly. First, you may benefit from knowing that Autistic researchers are interested in moving away from labels based on severity and functioning toward a more descriptive approach to differences and support needs. You might also reconsider using such terms yourself, especially if you do not know how the person you are talking to or about describes themself. Recalling our discussion in chapter 1 about how to talk about a student if you do not know their diagnosis or whether they are neurodivergent, using descriptive language instead of subjective severity or functioning labels may be helpful. If you are talking to a colleague about an Autistic student who is an accomplished writer, you could simply mention this detail rather than equating this strength with being "high functioning." If your class is watching a film in which one of the characters is Autistic and non-speaking or needs assistance with tasks such as personal care and transportation, you could describe them using those specific details instead of using terms like "low functioning" or "severe autism."

Second, this conversation might be helpful for thinking through other labels that we use for students, and how they may convey the misguided idea that the more different a student is from expectations, the worse they are. Along the lines of Dawson's example of blindness, I hope we would not say that a student is only "mildly" first generation if they seem to be able to navigate the customs, hidden curriculum challenges, and financial burdens of higher education comfortably, and that they are "severely" first generation if they also come from a low income family and experience significant difficulties navigating campus and academic life. However, it is certainly not uncommon to hear certain student groups described as monoliths or in ways that ignore a combination of strengths and challenges. As illustrated by the ransom notes campaign and the response to it, there is much to be gained by framing students' needs in a descriptive way, rather than using crisis narratives. One group of Autistic people historically associated with the "severe autism" category that researchers such as Dawson and Kapp have argued against are non-speaking or minimally speaking Autistics. More and more non-speaking students are entering higher education, and you may have taught students who use a text-to-speech device, iPad, or other form of augmentative and alternative communication (AAC).

Two notable minimally or non-speaking advocates that I have personally learned from are Hari Srinivasan and Jordyn Zimmerman. Srinivasan was previously the first minimally speaking president of the Spectrum: Autism at Cal club when he was an undergraduate student at the University of California, Berkeley. In an interview about his college experiences, he begins by saying that he was not expected to go to college at all, having largely been educated in segregated special education settings. When he did arrive at Cal, there was a major period of adjustment, especially in figuring out how to make friends.

> I did get to know other students over time and formed many friendships. I often had to educate them on how to include me. But Cal students were open to it and reached out, which makes all the difference. I found that I was being greeted by name when I walked around campus. To actually be known as "Hari" to many nondisabled folks was a totally new and absolutely heartwarming experience. At Cal, I studied psychology. I was able to engage in the most amazing conversations with every professor I had the opportunity to interact with. Disabled folks, especially significantly disabled ones like me, are not often afforded respect by educators.[21]

Zimmerman is a non-speaking disability advocate. Prior to her learning to type on an iPad around the age of 18, she was only able to communicate in a very limited way. After she started to use a device for communication, many more social and educational opportunities opened up for her. Among her many endeavors is sitting on the board of the organization CommunicationFIRST. Her work and that of CommunicationFIRST show the important overlaps between the Autistic community and other neurodivergent and disabled people who use non-spoken communication methods.

In an interview, she said about CommunicationFIRST that "the mission is to protect and advance the rights, autonomy, opportunity and dignity of people with speech-related disabilities . . . CommunicationFIRST is cross-disability, which is really important because whether someone is Autistic or has ALS [amyotrophic lateral sclerosis], our human rights and the discrimination that we face related to communication access is similar."[22] Through advocacy like Zimmerman's, Autistic people have become leaders in broader disability and human rights efforts, often drawing on their experiences of being misunderstood or undervalued.

The Emergence and Uses of the Term "Neurodivergent"

As the autism rights movement broadened, the term "neurodivergent" saw greater uptake, but its scope and precise meaning have also been contested. Learning some of this history and details of the debate can help us understand what students may mean when they identify as neurodivergent, and why a student with a mental disability may choose not to use that term for themself. As discussed in chapter 1, the term "neurodivergent" was coined in 2000 by online writer Kassiane Asasumasu. The term is another example of a neologism, like "neurotypical," that was first used in online communities and is now used widely in discussions of neurodiversity. Other writers have taken up the work of further defining and applying the term "neurodivergent," and I want to highlight two of them here. The first is Dr. Nick Walker, an Autistic psychologist and author of the book *Neuroqueer Heresies*. Walker discusses how he began broadening the concept of neurodivergence with Asasumasu's blessing (the two are friends) and sought to clarify its expansive nature.

> Neurodivergence is a value-neutral term that encompasses any significant divergence from dominant cultural norms of neurocognitive functioning . . . Unfortunately, as soon as the term started catching on, certain people started trying to redefine it more narrowly, in ways that directly violated Kassiane's inclusive intent. These people would often try to claim, for instance, that the term neurodivergence only referred to forms of neurodivergence that are innate genetic neurodevelopmental variants like autism.[23]

Walker goes on to say that it is preferable for "neurodivergent" to remain a broad and inclusive term, but that the specific needs of distinct groups under this umbrella deserve individual consideration. This is an important point for educators to remember. Let's say an instructor is interested in the experiences of dyslexic students. That instructor might form a focus group with dyslexic students or read some books about dyslexia and learn that these students can benefit from having text presented in particular typefaces or with specific spacing between letters.[24] Even though dyslexic students are neurodivergent, directly applying some of these strategies in an attempt to support all neurodivergent students might be misplaced.

The other writer I want to highlight is Sonny Jane Wise, who uses the professional moniker Lived Experience Educator. Wise, who is multiply neurodivergent, published the book *We're All Neurodiverse* in 2023.[25] They are the creator of the "neurodivergent umbrella" diagram, which helps to visualize what people mean when they say that "neurodiversity" or "neurodivergence" is an umbrella term. Wise makes several observations about the definition of "neurodivergence" that may be surprising. The first is that "neurodivergent" is a neutral term, not a positive or negative one. Wise writes that there is a broad misconception that for someone to identify as neurodivergent, they must view their divergence as a net positive or essential element of themselves, as some Autistic people do. Instead, Wise suggests that "neurodivergence" is only a description of how someone's mind diverges from norms, and individuals' relationships with their own neurodivergence can vary. Wise specifically includes people with mental health conditions or psychiatric disabilities in their definition. Furthermore, Wise argues that "neurodivergence" includes neurodivergent people who would desire a cure for their condition, as well as those who don't or who would oppose such a cure.

On the other side of the discussion, some neurodiversity researchers have suggested that the term "neurodivergent" may have either become overly broad or introduced confusion about whether neurodiversity advocates dislike the label "disabled." Researchers Ne'eman and Elizabeth Pellicano write, "After all, the commonsense interpretation of the creation of a special word to refer to neurological disability is that those who engage in such an act of creation find the latter term unacceptable in some way."[26] These authors suggest a slightly more conservative application of the neurodiversity concept (and implicitly the designation of "neurodivergent"): "the neurodiversity movement should seek to make itself relevant in those disability communities where a sufficient internal constituency exists for the application of the ideas of neurodiversity to their condition." One example of this principle playing out is the recent advocacy by people with Tourette's to have their condition understood as part of neurodiversity, as mentioned briefly in chapter 1.

Who considers themself neurodivergent and who does not remains a complex matter overall. Dana Lee Baker writes in her own book about the politics of neurodiversity:

> Just as happens with other characteristics more commonly associated with diversity, not everyone with a neurological difference identifies with neurodiverse communities. . . .
> A fundamental tenet of [her book] is that neurodiversity

> includes the right of individuals to choose not to publicly identify as having a neurological difference while simultaneously not supporting any social and political infrastructures that either universally encourage (or force) "passing" as neurologically typical, or incorporate negative consequences for publicly identifying as having a given neurological difference.[27]

Her point provides a useful coda for our discussion of the neurodiversity movement's interests and activities: Whether you personally do or do not identify as neurodivergent, we can all take steps to create environments where neurodivergent people are welcome and accepted.

Takeaways

Overall, this history of the autism rights and neurodiversity movements offers us useful lessons about the importance of relationships and respect over labels and assumptions. So many of the activities of the advocates discussed in this chapter were in response to feeling that they were not considered fully human because of their diagnoses. The next chapter explores the relationship between neurodiversity and disability, and we can now approach that discussion with an understanding of neurodivergence as a human condition, rather than an impersonal and presumptive label.

Teaching Invitations

- Reflect on how you can develop authentic relationships with students, including neurodivergent students, as whole people. Consider how focusing on students as people is an alternative to equating a person solely with their diagnosis.

- When discussing neurodivergent students, focus on their personhood, value, challenges, and growth opportunities, rather than only on deficits or labels.
- When referring to students' identities or disabilities, consider using neutral language if medical language is not required (e.g., Autistic vs. students with ASD).
- Be aware of assumptions about student deficits (e.g., "poor social skills"), which may be self-reinforcing.
- Consider applying aspects of the humanizing and accepting perspective offered by neurodiversity advocates to interactions with students and colleagues with mental health conditions, even if these individuals don't always identify as neurodivergent.

3

NEURODIVERSITY, DISABILITY, AND HIGHER ED

Neurodivergence and disability are partially overlapping but not equivalent categories. You may have noticed that this book is not subtitled *An Introduction to* ***Disability*** *for Educators*. Therefore, we have to do some work to explain the relevant overlaps and differences between disability and neurodivergence, and why an understanding of neurodiversity—as distinct from disability—is important for educators. This chapter will contribute to our neurodiversity literacy by considering how the neurodiversity movement is linked to the disability movement, how the categories of "disability" and "neurodivergence" overlap and diverge, and how variations in diagnosis and disclosure of disability may affect the experience of neurodivergence for students, staff, and instructors in higher education. It will also begin a discussion of how the concept of Universal Design—designing for the greatest number of people—interacts with neurodiversity.

Neurodiversity is a Part of Disability Rights

One important link between disability and neurodiversity is that neurodiversity advocates view themselves as aligned with disability rights. The ASAN is a leading neurodiversity movement organization, and it links itself explicitly to the disability rights conversation in its mission statement.[1] The statement reads, "The

Autistic Self Advocacy Network seeks to advance the principles of the disability rights movement with regard to autism. ASAN believes that the goal of autism advocacy should be a world in which autistic people enjoy equal access, rights, and opportunities," implying that equal access is a shared goal of disability rights and Autistic self-advocacy. Furthermore, the ASAN describes itself as "a national grassroots disability rights organization for the autistic community. We fight for disability rights. We work to make sure autistic people are included in policy-making, so that laws and policies meet our community's needs. We work to support all forms of self-advocacy and to change the way people think about autism." As we discussed in chapter 2, a common misconception about autism advocacy is that Autistic self-advocates do not consider autism to be a disability. This is not the case, and understanding why someone might recognize autism as a disability but not view it fundamentally as a pathology requires some context about disability rights.

Let's begin by situating neurodiversity within the wider context of disability, so that we may understand the relevant overlaps and differences. As we established in chapter 1, neurodiversity could be considered a basic fact about the human population—that naturally occurring cognitive variation exists among humans. The concept of neurodiversity, derived from conversations in the online Autistic community, laid the foundation for an understanding of cognitive differences that embraces diversity, rather than a view that all differences are by default pathological. Under the neurodiversity paradigm, there is no one right type of mind, and no form of cognitive difference is inherently pathological. However, most forms of neurodivergence could also be considered disabilities, depending on the exact definition and model of disability being used.

A disability could be defined as a condition that makes it more difficult to engage in certain activities in a given society. How the concept of disability should be specifically defined or understood is dependent on the model of disability being used. I like to tell my students that models of disability are different ways of viewing the root cause of disability and what the best response to a disability is. Two of the more commonly discussed models of disability are the medical model and the social model. The medical model views disability as a problem located within an individual, and the best response to disability as prevention of the disability before it occurs, and the provision of treatments and cures once it does occur. The medical model was primarily characterized and identified in the 1970s by disability rights activists in the UK who were searching for an alternative to the perspective that disability is an individual defect. Dana Lee Baker makes the useful point that the medical model was not developed or advanced by medical professionals; rather, it was posited by disability activists to explain the attitude of medical professionals toward disability.[2] The medical model of disability can be described as an essentialist model, meaning that any disability is regarded as a fundamental feature of an individual that can only be corrected by treating or curing the person.

The same disability rights activists introduced the social model of disability as an alternative to the prevailing medical model. The primary innovation of the social model was to separate impairment from disability.[3] If someone cannot move one of their legs, both the medical model and the social model would agree that they have an impairment. The medical model fully equates the impairment with disability: The person is disabled because they can't move their leg. The social model would instead describe their inability to move their leg as an impairment, but the difficulties they face in society as their disability. In short, the interaction between impairment and society produces a disability.

The way that the medical and social models of disability map on to neurodivergence is a matter of some debate among neurodivergent writers and researchers. Nick Walker offers one perspective, arguing that the medical model is aligned with what he calls the "pathology paradigm"—the idea that there is a "right" or "normal" human mind—and those that differ from this norm should be considered disordered.[4] In this view, the social model of disability aligns with the neurodiversity paradigm. Both frameworks suggest that individuals are not inherently disabled or disordered, and that social dynamics, rather than individual differences, are the main cause of disability and marginalization. Walker also contends that the social model can help explain disability that results from neurodivergence even when a person does not have any functional impairment. As an example, he imagines an Autistic person who "has no significant difficulty" with daily tasks or the demands of a job but does have a communication style and mannerisms that are noticeably Autistic.[5] Such a person might be considerably disabled in our society as a result of their differences and being noticeably Autistic because they face discrimination and social exclusion that make it difficult for them to work, learn, and live. Walker also notes that under a social model of disability, not all neurodivergent people are necessarily disabled. If we use a definition of "neurodivergence" that includes any and all cognitive differences that diverge from societal norms, it is easy to identify various forms of neurodivergence that differ from these norms but do not require accommodation or carry significant stigma. One example is synesthesia, an uncommon experience in which a person has overlapping sensory experiences such as associating words with certain colors, or sounds with particular sensations.[6]

Steven Kapp offers a contrasting perspective on how the medical and social models of disability relate to neurodiversity. Kapp contends that the neurodiversity movement has not necessarily taken the view that the medical model is completely irrelevant to neurodiversity.[7] Rather, the movement prioritizes "adaptive functioning" and overall "well-being" for neurodivergent people, whether the source of their challenges is primarily individual impairments or the inaccessibility of society. A number of Autistic researchers prefer an "interactionist" view of neurodivergence and disability (whereby individual impairments and societal conditions interact to produce disability) rather than a "strong social model," wherein societal conditions alone produce disability.[8] While the social model of disability is a useful tool for understanding how society is set up in ways that create barriers for disabled people, disability rights goals such as equal access and opportunity, and access to health care and education would still apply under other models.

I myself am a proponent of the interactionist perspective and believe it can be useful for educators in our work. An example that I like comes from Autistic researcher Patrick Dwyer, when he is explaining how the common Autistic trait of sound sensitivity causes disability. He notes that "hyperacusis [pain caused by hearing certain sounds] and loudness discomfort reflect internal neurobiological and perceptual differences, but they become disabling only when people's environments force them to expose themselves to distressing noise."[9] An instructor with knowledge of neurodivergent students' innate hearing differences might be moved to investigate how sound in their classroom can be modulated or dampened to support such students.

Invisible or Non-Apparent Disabilities and Neurodivergence

One additional distinction in the discourse about disability that is particularly relevant to neurodiversity and neurodivergence is that of apparent and non-apparent disabilities—whether one person's disability is perceptible to another person. These categories are often called "visible" and "invisible" disabilities, but I prefer the terms "apparent" and "non-apparent" for two reasons. First, the term "apparent" is inclusive of more senses than just sight, and this expansion seems appropriate in a discussion of disabilities. Second, "apparent" provides more room for flexibility in what is noticeable to an observer.

Often, the distinction between apparent and non-apparent disabilities is framed as whether there is a clear visual indicator of a disability (often physical), such as when someone uses a wheelchair or a cane. Thus, many mental disabilities are understood as non-apparent because others might not notice these when passing a person on the street or interacting with them briefly. However, whether a disability is known to someone else is also highly dependent on context. For example, a dyslexic student's disability might not be apparent to the security guard who they wave to on the way into a building on campus, but it might be more apparent to their classmates when the student reads a text out loud as part of a learning activity. A disability may also be much more apparent to a person who is familiar with that type of disability, or to someone who knows the person well (e.g., a family member of a person who becomes disabled as a result of an injury).

These categories have an unusual relationship to neurodiversity and neurodivergence. As we noted in chapter 1, describing someone as "neurodivergent" means that their cognition differs from societal norms, and that this may be linked to a specific diagnosis of disability, multiple such diagnoses, or no diagnosis at all. Because most of the disabilities associated with neurodivergence are mental disabilities, neurodivergent people are often said to have invisible or non-apparent disabilities. In fact, two noteworthy books that discuss the needs and experiences of neurodivergent students reference invisible disabilities in their titles.[10] However, many neurodivergent people do communicate or behave in ways that are different from the majority of people, and these differences can be readily apparent. For example, some Autistic people use text-based communication all or some of the time. Dyspraxic people may move in ways that differ from non-dyspraxic people. As discussed in chapters 1 and 2, people with Tourette's usually have noticeable tics. Ash Lierman writes that one way of understanding "invisible disabilities" is that they are both less likely to be apparent to observers than other types of disabilities (like physical or sensory ones) and relatedly are also likely to draw the most skepticism about their legitimacy.[11] My own preferred way of relating neurodivergence to the categories of apparent and non-apparent disabilities is to say that many disabilities that are associated with neurodivergence are "less apparent" disabilities. They are perhaps less likely than some physical disabilities to be noticed in a brief interaction but are often apparent in the context of a relationship.

Disability Law and Neurodiversity

Under US law, students with disabilities are protected under two main laws: Section 504 of the Rehabilitation Act, and the ADA, passed in 1973 and 1990 respectively. Both of these two laws prohibit discrimination on the basis of disability but apply to different types of institutions. Section 504 prohibits exclusion on the basis of disability from any program or activity that receives federal assistance. This covers just about all colleges and universities in the country because of federal student financial aid. The ADA, on the other hand, prohibits discrimination on the basis of disability in any publicly funded institution of higher education. Functionally, Section 504 applies to both private and public institutions, but the ADA has more effect on public ones (such as community colleges and state institutions) through its Title II requirements. For example, a new rule for Title II of the ADA was implemented in 2024 that requires digital materials produced by public entities (including public institutions of higher education) to be accessible to people with disabilities. Though there is uncertainty about how this rule will be enforced on an ongoing basis, it would in theory only apply to public institutions and not private colleges and universities.

Another important law to know about in the context of neurodiversity is the Individuals with Disabilities in Education Act (IDEA), which applies to K-12 education. It came into effect in 1990, the same year that the ADA was passed. The law requires that students with disabilities have access to a "free and appropriate education" (FAPE) in the "least restrictive environment" (LRE).[12] These two terms are worth unpacking because of their relevance to neurodivergent students. The "free" part of FAPE means that students with disabilities cannot be excluded from free public education because of their disability, and in some cases a school district is obligated to pay for private education if it cannot accommodate a student with disabilities. The "appropriate" component of FAPE means that students with disabilities must have access to challenging curricula that are appropriate for their needs and abilities. Prior to IDEA, students with disabilities would routinely be provided with substandard educational options, often based on stereotypes and generalizations about their abilities and future goals. My students are usually shocked when we watch celebrated disability rights activist Judy Heumann's TED Talk in which she recalls that the New York City Department of Education sent a teacher to her home only twice a week while her school was not wheelchair accessible, and the teacher taught her cross-stitch rather than academic subjects.[13] The LRE component of IDEA deals with the issue of segregation. Under IDEA, students are entitled to a learning environment that is as integrated with nondisabled students as possible. IDEA was inspired by and modeled after *Brown v. Board of Education*, the Supreme Court decision that made racial segregation in schools illegal. The act is based on the principle that students with disabilities do not receive an equal education when they are segregated in separate classrooms from nondisabled students. The effects of IDEA since its implementation have been quite significant for students and their families, but I want to briefly address the specific effects of IDEA on higher education. Students with disabilities' increased access to education under IDEA has led to greater academic success for these students in elementary and high school, and in turn to larger numbers of them applying to and enrolling in college. Compared to past decades, the increased number of neurodivergent students—especially those with autism, ADHD, and learning disabilities—on campuses today may reflect the success of inclusive policy at the K-12 level. Even though there are significant differences in how a disabled student will navigate higher education from K-12, students with disabilities are likely to arrive in college with some knowledge of what accommodations and services they need to support them. Additionally, most nondisabled students who went through their earlier education during the IDEA era have experience of learning alongside students with disabilities. These are all welcome developments for neurodivergent students.

When students with documented disabilities engage with a disability services office, they can access a range of services and accommodations depending on the specific nature of their disability. Students go through an interactive process with the disability services staff that ideally results in accommodations that are tailored to the specific nature of the student's disability and the way that it affects their academic participation. These types of accommodations are important—indeed in many cases essential—for disabled students attempting to access higher education. Except in rare cases, such accommodations require medical documentation of a disability. Walker notes that the accommodations system is thus informed by the medical model of disability and the pathology paradigm: One must receive a medical diagnosis and disclose it in order to receive accommodations, and these accommodations are applied to individuals because of their disabilities.[14] In keeping with the pathology paradigm, a student who is neurodivergent must first be labeled as disordered in some way before they can receive an accommodation, rather than having the opportunity to state their needs and have them respectfully considered without such a label.

The issues around disclosure and privacy are significant when navigating disability in higher education. Accordingly, I want to address two very important ways that neurodiversity manifests in higher education, and in our lives more generally: through an undisclosed diagnosis, and through no diagnosis at all. We touched on the topics of self-diagnosis and lack of diagnosis in chapter 1 when we discussed how we define and operationalize the category of "neurodivergence." However, there is still important ground to cover regarding how these manifestations of neurodiversity interact with rights, law, and policy in higher ed.

To review, here are some potential reasons that someone who is neurodivergent may not disclose a specific disability:

- The person fears adverse judgment because of stigma about their disability—for example, a student who has been viewed negatively in the past for having a learning disability.
- The diagnosis is new, or the person doesn't have sufficient information about it, leading to uncertainty about how to advocate for themselves. For example, a staff colleague in your office has been recently diagnosed with ADHD but is not sure what this diagnosis means for her professional life. She is planning to share her diagnosis at a later date when she knows what support she wants to request.
- There is an additional burden involved in disclosing a disability and requesting accommodations (also sometimes called a "disability tax").[15] This process takes time and energy, and the person may not have that time or feel that they want to spend their limited time on this. For example, a graduate student with a mental disability in your department has an upcoming qualifying exam. On hearing from a more senior student that the process of documenting her disability and requesting accommodations required multiple appointments and several weeks' waiting time, he decides to focus his efforts on studying for the exam, hoping that accommodations won't be necessary.
- The person has no diagnosis at all but still identifies as neurodivergent.

In addition to situations in which someone does not disclose a disability at all, it is common for instructors to not know the specific disability that a student has when they request accommodations.

While the disability services office needs to know the specific nature of any disability in order to determine appropriate accommodations, this is considered to be private medical information and will not be shared with the instructor. Thus, because "neurodivergence" is not a biomedical term and there are multiple factors impacting diagnosis and disclosure, it is possible to say that many neurodivergent students will be eligible for disability services, but not all will be. There are also complex situations in which a person might reveal their diagnosis to certain people but not others, and in which an individual's neurodivergence is more apparent to some people than it is to others. Instead of simply saying, "It's complicated" and moving on, let's explore this complexity a bit further.

Beyond Diagnosed and Undiagnosed: Neurodiversity Personas

The following four vignettes are designed to demonstrate the complexity of how neurodiversity interacts with disability in higher education. I call these fictional characters "composite personas" because their stories are not strictly hypothetical; rather they are based on real details from my own academic journey and those of students and colleagues. After each profile, I offer some analysis and recommendations for how the subject of the story could apply their neurodiversity literacy to the scenario. As you read, you can keep an eye out for the themes of disclosure of disability without engagement with disability services, self-identification without medical diagnosis, and students and colleagues who we might think of as neurodivergent but who don't use that label for themselves.

Charlotte

Charlotte is a second-year student in an engineering program at a state university. You are her instructor for a course in her major, and you are meeting during student hours in your office. While discussing an upcoming assignment, she tells you that she has ADHD in the context of her efforts to set personal deadlines to complete certain parts of the project. "If I don't have deadlines, there is no way I am going to work on this ahead of time." You are surprised, since you didn't receive the customary letter from disability services at the beginning of the semester to indicate that Charlotte is entitled to accommodations. You respond warmly, saying, "Thanks for sharing that. It sounds like you have a good idea of how you can be successful with this assignment, but I also want to make myself available if I can provide any other support."

ANALYSIS AND RECOMMENDATIONS

This student likely has a diagnosis that is associated with neurodivergence (in this case ADHD), which she has disclosed to you, though there is a chance that she could be self-diagnosed or self-identified. There are a number of possibilities why you never received a letter from disability services on Charlotte's behalf. One is that she is not registered with disability services at all, having chosen not to go through that process, or is self-identified and therefore not eligible for accommodations. Another possibility is that your disability services office allows students to decide whether a letter gets sent to individual instructors. Charlotte may have felt that the accommodations she is entitled to, such as extra time on exams, were not necessary for this class because you do not give your students timed assessments. Your response is supportive and recognizes Charlotte's agency and self-advocacy abilities. Because Charlotte has disclosed a disability to you, in the future you could easily recommend that she work with disability services if barriers arise that could be mitigated with accommodations. If you keep notes from student meetings, you could write down both that Charlotte disclosed having ADHD and that clear due dates support her time management. In summary, Charlotte is neurodivergent, and you as the instructor do not know whether she has a formal diagnosis of ADHD or is registered with disability services.

Marvin

Marvin is a midcareer scholar in your department, who has been active in sociology research for over a decade. He has taught most of the department's offerings at least once, though you notice he has only been teaching one online course per semester over the last year. During a casual conversation with one of your other colleagues, Jade, you wonder aloud whether work on a new book or travel for research has caused this change in Marvin's teaching load. Jade says they heard that Marvin is having some health problems as a result of a car accident. You seem to remember Marvin saying that this accident wasn't too serious, and he was lucky not to be badly injured—he just had a concussion. However, you also recall that brain injuries such as concussions can cause lasting cognitive symptoms.

ANALYSIS AND RECOMMENDATIONS

If Jade is correct that the residual effects of an injury are affecting Marvin and his work, we might say that he has a cognitive disability as a result of this injury, and that he could now be considered neurodivergent. This composite persona provides a useful note that neurodivergence is not always the result of a developmental or psychiatric disability. Someone's cognitive function can diverge from expected norms because of an injury, illness, surgery, or medical event such as a stroke or heart attack. Matthew Hora gives an excellent first-person account of navigating academia with a disability resulting from an injury in his essay on working as a faculty member with a traumatic brain injury.[16] These types of disabilities and neurodivergence might be destabilizing both for the affected person and for their colleagues, in part because they begin so quickly and require a sudden adjustment of expectations. The change may be especially pronounced if the person previously fit very well within the norms and expectations of academic life (teaching multiple courses per semester, publishing research, traveling to campus and other locations). If Marvin has ongoing effects from a concussion, he may be dealing with sensory sensitivities, difficulty reading, or other cognitive impairments, and he may have requested a reduced teaching load as an accommodation.

As this scenario doesn't directly involve Marvin, you might not have an opportunity to discuss this matter with him. This story can, however, serve as a reminder that a student or colleague may become neurodivergent as a result of a one-off event like an accident or illness. Even though the neurodiversity movement originally focused on cognitive differences like autism that are developmental and lifelong, the expansion of the category of neurodivergence to encompass any experience of cognitive function that does not align with societal expectations could cover an injury such as Marvin's. His disability affects his capacity to work, and he has likely negotiated a reduced workload. Disability studies scholar Susan Wendell writes about how the social construction of disability is significantly affected by the "pace of life," or the expectations about how much a person can accomplish in a given amount of time.[17] As an ally for neurodivergent people, rather than question Marvin's change in capacity, you might want to respect it and encourage colleagues to do the same. For example, if a coworker asks when Marvin will "be back to normal," you might say that you know his capacity has changed and the reduction in his teaching load may be permanent. You could engage your colleagues in a conversation about collective efforts to serve the department's students rather than focusing on Marvin.

C. J.

You are an instructor of marketing in an undergraduate school of business. A student named C. J. was in one of your courses last semester and was an excellent student from your perspective. C. J. appeared engaged during class, sitting near the front and asking several questions during each session. Their knowledge and skills were clearly valued by their teammates during a group assignment in which the students had to develop a marketing plan for a campus restaurant. Looking over the roster for the upcoming semester, you are delighted to see that you will be teaching C. J. again. On the first day of class, C. J. is seated in the front row as usual. Today, they are wearing a T-shirt that reads, "Proud to be Autistic." You didn't know that C. J. was Autistic and are surprised. You remember that you knew C. J. had some sort of disability, because you received an accommodation letter from disability services stating that C. J. would be permitted to use noise-canceling headphones during exams. However, you didn't know what kind of disability that accommodation related to. You know that Autistic people are not a monolith but that they might struggle with social communication and understanding social norms. From your perspective, C. J. isn't observably distinct from their peers in their social interactions except that you have noticed some differences in their use of eye contact in conversation.

ANALYSIS AND RECOMMENDATIONS

Your interactions with C. J. help to illustrate a few important points about apparent and non-apparent disabilities. Neurodivergence in particular is often a non-apparent disability because cognitive differences usually manifest in a person's thinking, behavior, and communication—things that are not always apparent from encountering a person for a short period of time. There are a few potential reasons why you might not have known that C. J. is Autistic until they came to school wearing the "Proud to be Autistic" shirt. One may be that autism affects C. J. in ways that other people don't often notice—C. J. may engage with special interests outside the school day, or stim in a less visible way or not at all. Another possibility is that C. J. masks some of their Autistic traits in academic environments. "Masking" refers to attempts to hide or diminish certain traits of neurodivergence or another disability in order to fit in to a particular situation or avoid stigma.

There may be no need to bring up your newfound knowledge that C. J. is Autistic, but an opportunity may arise to demonstrate your allyship if you want to. For example, if C. J. happens to mention any particular needs or difficulties that might be related to their neurodivergence, you could explain that you noticed their "Proud to be Autistic" shirt and are always available to chat about their experiences on your campus. More broadly, you might use this as a reminder that neurodivergence is not always apparent in a given context. In this situation, C. J. did have some noticeably neurodivergent traits, but you only realized they were neurodivergent traits once you knew that C. J. was Autistic. It behooves instructors not to make blanket assumptions that there aren't any neurodivergent students in their classes without knowing for certain.

Bella

You are the instructor of record for a large undergraduate economics course and supervise a team of eight graduate teaching assistants (TAs). You hold a weekly meeting with them where you discuss the content and activities for the week and collaborate on lesson plans for the discussion sections that the TAs lead. Bella is an enthusiastic TA who is interested in finding a teaching-intensive faculty position in the future. She experiences significant anxiety, which affects her participation in the team meetings, and has privately discussed with you her diagnosis and pursuit of treatment. During one of your conversations, you mention some ideas from a seminar on embracing neurodiversity in the classroom that you hope to integrate into the TA team meetings. These include offering the option to contribute to discussions either verbally or by adding to a shared document. Bella appreciates the ideas and thinks that she will be able to share her views more thoroughly with the text-based option. However, she expresses dismay that these ideas so often seem to be raised with reference to students who are neurodivergent—a label she doesn't identify with.

ANALYSIS AND RECOMMENDATIONS

As discussed in chapters 1 and 2, neurodiversity and neurodivergence are potentially broad concepts, and not everyone with cognitive differences or disabilities may personally identify with them. Bella's disability—anxiety, or "generalized anxiety disorder" in medical language—fits under the umbrella of neurodivergence in some conceptions. For example, Sonny Jane Wise's broad definition of "neurodivergence" includes both people who experience their conditions as a neutral or positive part of themselves and don't desire curative treatment, and those who experience their conditions as distressing and do desire a cure.[18] Nevertheless, Bella doesn't find "neurodivergent" to be a useful term for herself. Her openness about her perspective provides two opportunities. First, you could state your respect for her rejection of the label "neurodivergent" for herself, and ask more about how she does conceptualize her anxiety. Second, when you discuss promoting inclusivity in the future, you could take care to recognize that not all people with mental disabilities identify with categories within neurodivergence. For example, you might say, "I was thinking we could incorporate several types of participation into our meetings. I expect that this could help a range of different students, including students with disabilities or mental health conditions, neurodivergent students, and any other students for whom verbal participation might not be ideal."

Hopefully these personas and analyses have helped to demonstrate that the relationships between neurodivergence, disability, and disclosure are far from simple. Let's now build on this discussion to highlight how another major innovation in disability advocacy, Universal Design, relates to neurodiversity.

Accommodations and Universal Design: Opportunities and Caveats

One of the most significant contributions of the disability rights movement has been the introduction of Universal Design—an approach to design that aims to make environments as accessible as possible to the greatest number of people. From my own perspective, the opportunities and caveats of Universal Design for teaching that is responsive to neurodiversity are so significant that this chapter and chapters 4 and 5 all contain extended discussions of aspects of this approach. Designing learning environments to be as accessible as possible to the largest number of people is one of the most worthwhile goals I can imagine. Because this objective is also incredibly complex, the application of one or more Universal Design principles rarely results in access for all. So, throughout this book, I take a decidedly non-utopian perspective on Universal Design. I phrase my approach as "non-utopian" because I believe both that Universal Design is critical to neurodiversity-affirming teaching and that it is not a panacea.

In this chapter, I primarily discuss Universal Design as a broad approach to accessible design, and focus on one of its seven principles that I believe is understudied and underapplied in education: tolerance for error. Chapters 4 and 5 discuss more of the history of the specific UDL framework, the most popular application of Universal Design in education. Universal Design was initially conceptualized as an approach to accessible design for buildings so that they could be navigated by people with and without disabilities. Ron Mace, an architect and wheelchair user who developed the ideas, aimed to offer an approach to design that diverged from retrofitting buildings for access, which the public tended to view as costly and unsightly.[19] The following principles are set out by the Center for Excellence in Universal Design:

- Equitable use: The design is useful and marketable to people with diverse abilities.

- Flexibility in use: The design accommodates a wide range of individual preferences and abilities.
- Simple and intuitive use: Use of the design is easy to understand regardless of the user's experience, knowledge, language skills, or current level of concentration.
- Perceptible information: The design communicates necessary information effectively to the user, regardless of ambient conditions or the user's sensory abilities.
- Tolerance for error: The design minimizes hazards and the adverse consequences of accidental or unintentional actions.
- Low physical effort: The design can be used efficiently and comfortably with a minimum amount of fatigue.
- Size and space for approach and use: Appropriate size and space are provided for approach, reach, manipulation, and use regardless of the user's body size, posture, or mobility.[20]

Reviewing these principles, we can see that Universal Design deals not only with initial access to a building or space—such as an entrance ramp—but also navigation of that space and use of objects within it. It is easy to think about access as just about getting in the front door of some physical or metaphorical place, but the Universal Design principles center "use" of the design in an ongoing negotiation. While these principles are often regarded as ways to think about physical accessibility, a close reading of them shows that they also refer to cognition and the senses, highlighting the perceptibility of information and usability of the design regardless of "knowledge, language skills, or current level of concentration." These considerations make a specific connection to mental disabilities and indirectly to neurodiversity.

However, the principles of Universal Design as developed by Mace are rarely directly applied to learning contexts. UDL—the framework developed by special education researchers and currently stewarded by the organization CAST—uses the idea of accessibility with fewer retrofits as its starting point but has evolved to take into account research on learning and cognitive science.[21] The UDL framework includes its own set of guidelines which are separate from the principles of Universal Design. Universal Design for Instruction is another framework for incorporating Universal Design into education, which builds on ideas from UDL and web accessibility guidelines, as well as the original principles of Universal Design.[22] Here, I want to use one of these original principles to make a point about how accommodations cannot always address the challenges that neurodivergent students encounter. Neurodiversity could be said to exist in tension with the accommodations model of disability access in higher education for several reasons.

- Neurodiversity is not always captured by a medical diagnosis.
- Neurodivergent people have a range of relationships to "disability" as a category.
- Neurodivergence may become more apparent or more consequential in specific learning situations.
- Interactions in a neurodiverse group often involve some differences in communication or information processing that can result in misunderstandings between people. These misunderstandings may be better addressed using ideas about flexibility rather than accommodations.

One of the goals of Universal Design is to create designs that can be used by the greatest number of people without or with less reliance on retrofitting. I believe that one important consideration about Universal Design and disability is that for many situations that involve neurodiversity, accommodations may not appropriately address needs that emerge contextually (i.e., in a specific learning activity) or as a result of communication and processing differences. To examine how Universal Design can facilitate access in ways that accommodations often cannot, let's explore the principle of "tolerance for error."

Tolerance for Error

In the context of architectural or product design, "tolerance for error" means that differences or mistakes in how people use something will not affect the overall function. Some examples of tolerance for error in products are multiple ways to grip an object, a doorknob working when pushed or turned in either direction, or a door swinging both ways. A user will not be met with an adverse consequence as a result of pushing the door in the "wrong" way. Another process that helps show how tolerance for error can be integrated into design is that of entering a password for an online account, which many of us do several times per day. Tolerance for error sometimes needs to be balanced with other concerns, in this case password security. There are already a number of features built into most authentication systems that are designed to promote security, such as replacing the characters with dots as you type them, so that someone looking over your shoulder cannot read your password, and temporarily locking the password system if too many wrong passwords are entered (as this resembles some hacking attempts). These are balanced with features demonstrating tolerance for error, such as allowing the user to "reveal" their password before entering it (usually by pressing an icon shaped like an eye), making multiple attempts to enter a password before locking the system, and providing a way to recover a lost or forgotten password.

The phrase "tolerance for error" does connote that there are "erroneous" uses of a product or space. However, Jay Dolmage, in his book *Academic Ableism*, offers an interpretation of this principle that avoids labeling differences as "errors" and provides a useful link to the neurodiversity paradigm: Designing for tolerance for error is also a way of saying that there are "many ways to be right."[23] For example, password entry systems increasingly provide multiple ways to log in, such as sending a code to a phone or email, as a default instead of only after repeated errors in entering the password. We would say that this transition is an example of extending tolerance for error to "many ways to be right." This perspective connects to the neurodiversity paradigm because it suggests that we think beyond one right way to do something, whether in the classroom or any other context. Even when "error" is the most appropriate way to describe a misstep or difference in understanding, building in tolerance for error helps to frame errors as learning opportunities.[24]

Much of the discussion around Universal Design in education happens in the context of UDL, which frames the different ways that students engage in the learning process or demonstrate their knowledge in terms of available options and proactive design. For instance, how could we design an assessment that does not assume students express themselves best through writing? Universal Design perspectives in education rarely address how we can mitigate the consequences of unintentional actions. For example, in accessibility expert Sheryl Burgstahler's well-known checklist of Universal Design strategies—incorporating both general Universal Design principles and UDL principles—tolerance for error is only referenced twice.[25] I develop tolerance for error as it relates to teaching in this chapter for two reasons.

1. In keeping with the original intent of Universal Design, I want to offer a concrete example of how the concept may support neurodivergent students' success in ways that are not typically addressed through the accommodations process. This means recognizing that barriers exist not only in the initial design or framing of learning experiences but also in intolerance for mistakes and differences in understanding that occur through the learning process.
2. The concept of Universal Design—as we will explore through the principle of tolerance for error—makes an important link between some of the themes of neurodiversity advocacy and disability advocacy. Environments

> are less disabling when there is a combination of tolerance for error and multiple ways to be right.

I initially conceptualized these connections after trying to reflect on my own teaching practices, which are informed by some of my personal experiences as a neurodivergent student and other observations of how students have been left out or faced adverse consequences in the learning environment. As Kelly Hogan and Viji Sathy observe, students might be excluded if an inclusive approach is not adopted.[26] Here is an example based on my grading and assessment approach. I attempt to offer the most detailed descriptions possible of my expectations for assignments, as well as the range of variability that is acceptable. I might require that students cite five or more peer-reviewed articles, and I would specify that these articles could come from different disciplines. If students are writing about a particular disability, they could cite peer-reviewed articles from both medical journals and disability studies journals. If a student submits their assignment and I notice a significant gap between their work and my expectations (e.g., they have not cited the required number of peer-reviewed articles), the first thing I do is send them a note to explain that their assignment doesn't meet the expectations and why. I also ask if they would like to revise it. From my perspective, there are a lot of things that could have led to this error, including the student misunderstanding the assignment or mistakenly submitting an early draft instead of a finished version. Almost all students to whom I send this message do revise their first attempt. When I describe this practice to colleagues and friends, I often get the response that it seems extremely (if not overly) generous.

In reflecting on why I naturally gravitate toward this approach, I was able to identify that it is derived from a lot of my own early experiences as a student and instructor. As I mentioned earlier in this chapter, clarifying expectations as much as possible is a near-ubiquitous piece of teaching advice. In addition to being a recommended practice for supporting neurodivergent students, it is also thought to support first-generation and international students.[27] The practice also aligns with the Universal Design principle of simple and intuitive use. However, this effort does not always go as planned. Consider an anecdote from a study on faculty perceptions of working with Autistic students,[28] also referenced by Kuder et al.[29] The study found that Autistic students struggle with "audience recognition" or "a lack of awareness of the mindset of others."[30]

> In the words of one instructor reflecting on the challenge inherent in writing assignments, "When we talk about writing we frequently ask students to think about the needs of their audience . . . and the audience is not always the person sitting in front of them or their teacher. It becomes a challenge to think about anyone other than themselves." In another example, a respondent recounted guiding a student to include more rationale and procedural information in his lab report. The student was reluctant to do so because the teacher "already knew" what the experiment was all about. In this case, he did not imagine or write for an audience who did not share his background knowledge.[31]

This anecdote caught my attention because it is exactly the sort of situation I would have found myself in as a student. From my perspective, there is a value-neutral discrepancy between how the instructor and student view the tasks. The instructor likely wants the student to practice the kind of writing used in journal articles (in which you can't assume the reader has background knowledge of the study). The student is thinking of the assignment more in terms of its literal function—it is a report that a student writes for an instructor about the results of their experiment. The article somewhat strangely categorizes this situation as an example of the Autistic student's deficit in perspective taking, because they didn't think about a reader who didn't know the background of the experiment. The student surely demonstrates some perspective taking—correctly noting that the instructor is not likely to need background information about the experiment—but perhaps not the type desired.

Even if we say that this is a neutral conflict of understanding about the audience, in practice this is not how these situations tend to be treated. Often when I had this type of difference in understanding from my instructors, I would receive a low grade on the lab report—frequently as the result of two or three such misunderstandings on a single assignment. In a class that had only four lab reports in a semester, a grade such as 40 percent was hard to come back from. It seems to me that a companion strategy to clarifying all expectations is to adopt more humility about one's own perspective as an instructor, and create space where understanding can be reached about expectations without serious consequences. However, this can mean that instructors have to commit to interpreting these misunderstandings as something to resolve, rather than punish. A lot would have changed for me academically if I had had more opportunities to receive the feedback that I had not met expectations without it being accompanied by a catastrophically low grade.

UDL proponent Jennifer Katz suggests that tolerance for error in an educational context means that "both instruction and assessment recognize differences in student comprehension, pace of learning, and need for repetitions of the instructions along with the actions."[32] This understanding of tolerance for error takes into account student differences that are commonly associated with neurodivergence. Tolerance for error may make an important contribution to the success of neurodivergent students because it addresses situations that are typically not covered by existing accommodations. To review, some of the more common accommodations for neurodivergent students include:

- access to support with note taking
- assistive devices and other assistive technologies

- extended or flexible time for assignments and assessments
- instructions communicated in writing rather than verbally
- environments with reduced distraction for certain activities

These accommodations address access but do not address errors, mistakes, or differences in the learning process that may affect neurodivergent students adversely. In addition, a host of other students may be likely to make such errors and experience serious consequences. In Katz's description, these are differences in comprehension, pace, and need for repetition that may not be apparent earlier in the learning process but may only be revealed later. This links to our discussion of how apparent and non-apparent disabilities relate to neurodivergence. I think the anecdotes about my own lab reports and the student who understood the audience of his writing to be his expert instructor offer examples of how many forms of neurodivergence are less apparent at first but become more apparent as communication, learning, and assessment unfold.

In the account of the student who was having difficulty with the instruction to describe his experiment in full in his lab report, the struggle that occurred did not seem to be caused by a lack of initial "access." The instructor may have been willing to provide additional detail about the assignment ahead of submission, provide flexibility on due dates, and so on. Nonetheless, the differences in comprehension inherent in the interaction still needed to be resolved through reaching a shared understanding about the audience and objectives of a lab report. The application of tolerance for error here could mean providing the student with an opportunity to revise his work or turn in another version of the assignment with updated background on the experiment. Another application of tolerance for error could be accepting the student's work as is and recognizing that greater explanation and discussion of the audience will be needed for future assignments. Any approach that acknowledges that perfect understanding is an unreasonable goal and values students' attempts to meet expectations, even if they do not do so perfectly, could reasonably be described as "tolerance for error."

As we further explore higher education's structural factors and how they interact with neurodiversity, the principle of "more than one way to be right" will become increasingly relevant in our discussions of teaching practices. The neurodiversity paradigm's contention that there is no inherently right way to think, behave, or communicate would likely lead us to say that there is no inherently right way to teach or learn either. Chapter 4 will offer a closer look at the way that higher education often does take a "one right way" perspective, and the opportunities and challenges of questioning that tendency.

Takeaways

This chapter begins our discussion of the immense complexity of responding to neurodiversity as instructors. Neurodiversity overlaps and interacts with disability as a category: Many forms of neurodivergence are also disabilities, under both the medical and social models of disability. The neurodiversity paradigm aligns with the social model of disability, in that it recognizes that the interaction of individuals' essential differences with societal norms and structures produces barriers for neurodivergent people. Neurodivergence sometimes manifests as an invisible or non-apparent disability, but certain forms of neurodivergence, like Tourette's, are more apparent, while others may be more apparent in certain contexts (e.g., learning environments). As we continue to explore neurodiversity in academic environments, we can keep in mind that if we start from a place of curiosity, the wide scope of neurodiversity is likely to become more and more "apparent" to us.

Teaching Invitations

- If you teach about disability rights and history, consider including the activities of the neurodiversity movement in your teaching—neurodiversity advocates are part of the disability rights movement.
- If students disclose a disability to you, consider asking if particular methods of support have been helpful to them in the past. If you are in the United States, students are likely to have received some type of support or accommodations under Section 504, the ADA, or IDEA.
- Neurodivergence may be more or less apparent depending on context. It might be a good idea to avoid assumptions about whether students and colleagues are neurotypical or neurodivergent.
- Remember that the relationship between disability, disclosure, and neurodiversity is complex. Since not all people with mental disabilities identify as neurodivergent, you might avoid using this categorization as a stand-in for all mental disabilities.
- Consider that students who fail to meet certain expectations do not always do so out of ignorance but because of differences in understanding.
- Consider the opportunities tolerance for error can provide in your own teaching context—do mistakes or errors have any adverse consequences that you would like to prevent?

4

NORMAL SCHOOLS?

The Pathology and Neurodiversity Paradigms in Higher Education

One of the ways I commonly discuss neurodiversity with instructors and other staff in higher education is through guest talks. Attendees are often very interested in the terms and histories that we have explored so far in this book and are equally interested in ways that they can support neurodivergent students. Here is one of the ways I begin the discussion: I encourage participants to recall that the neurodiversity paradigm opposes the idea of a normal and abnormal brain—and learner. I also remind them to note that "neurotypical" and "neurodivergent" are sociopolitical concepts, because they describe how people's cognition does or doesn't conform to societal standards or expectations. I then ask, "How is the idea of 'normality' present in our classrooms and educational systems more broadly?" Participants are almost always able to offer incisive analysis on this topic with no preparation. This is true even of those who were drawn to the session specifically because they feel unequipped to address the needs of the growing number of neurodivergent students in their classrooms. I've paraphrased several of the most common responses below.

- Strict and inflexible deadlines are a major expression of normality. In fact, the ways that we enforce normality through due dates goes even beyond typical workplace expectations, where quality work is often valued over an exact delivery date. Not only that, but we don't even use these norms in scholarly work! Deadlines are regularly extended, and extensions and delays are commonplace.

- The course load expected of students is an expression of normality—in many ways the need to take 12–15 credits per semester is totally arbitrary, but because it is a norm, a student who "succeeds" in getting good grades with this course load is considered a good one, and a student who doesn't is considered a bad one. These bad students are punished, with lower GPAs, and risks to their financial aid and academic progress.
- Normality is expressed in the assumption of prose writing as the main form of communication in academic assignments. There are so many other ways to communicate or show knowledge, but essays are always the default.

I could list many more, but I want to stress that these are spontaneously generated examples of the problems of normality in higher education. There are large and ever-increasing numbers of popular and scholarly books that describe in detail the exclusionary nature of higher education, from admissions[1] to costs and student debt,[2] to the punitive and arbitrary grading systems we use,[3] to the poor overall working conditions for instructors which contribute to poor student learning conditions.[4] The works cited in the endnotes are important texts which have helped shape my own thinking about the norms of higher education. Money, prior academic success and status, and the ability to learn and demonstrate knowledge in a way that fits with the prevailing assessment approaches all facilitate a smooth journey through the current version of higher education. Lacking any of these things impedes a student's progress. I am always struck by how readily workshop participants can supply their own examples of normality, such as the ones mentioned above, often using personal experiences or anecdotes from their students. These participant examples are less *arguments* about the normative nature of the higher education system that we inhabit than direct experiences of it.

Perhaps instructors are (as a group) acutely aware of the norms of higher education because we are often responsible for upholding them. One of the anecdotes I offered in the introduction to this book was that schools for teacher preparation used to be called "normal schools." I recalled this fact while reading an article by neurodivergent academic Peter Smagorinsky called, "Neurodiversity and the Deep Structure of Schools."[5] He observes that "The name of 'Normal Schools' for teacher training was deliberate. They were established to instill norms in teachers, students, schools, curriculum, and instruction to serve the end of social stability."[6] While the names of these schools have almost all been changed, it is still impossible to deny that we as teachers are products and agents of a normative system.

Teachers and the Pathology Paradigm

Disability studies scholars Sharon Snyder and David Mitchell write that educators are among the "controlling professions"—a broad group of professionals who define, oversee, and often surveil disability—as are doctors, psychiatrists, and agents of mental health services.[7] Their point is not necessarily that these professionals always exert control over individuals (though they absolutely do at times), but that they control the narrative around pathology and normality. As Snyder and Mitchell suggest, adherence to the pathology paradigm and medical model of disability is not by any means limited to the medical community. The model is dubbed "medical" more as a description of how disability is *medicalized*, rather than referring to the model's relationship to doctors specifically.

When I first read this description of teachers as controlling professionals, I was stung. As a neurodivergent teacher who advocates for inclusion and designs my courses to be maximally accessible to disabled students, I bristled at being labeled one of the "bad actors." But after pushing past this initial reaction, I have come to recognize that it is important to understand and respond to the theory that teaching is—at least sometimes—a controlling profession. Teachers often do uphold the pathology paradigm, sometimes deliberately but often as a necessity, or due to a lack of other options. Here are a few examples of how educators may do this. I use the term "we" in these to include myself, since all instructors will probably uphold the pathology paradigm from time to time.

- While we are not responsible for making diagnoses, we often require them so students can receive support, flexibility, and accommodations—and this requires students to spend money and time on appointments and evaluations. This system suggests that the normal way to proceed through a class is without any adjustment or negotiation, and students with abnormal needs must adequately document a disability to be able to request accommodations. A neurodiversity paradigm approach would likely presume that different needs for support, flexibility, and adjustments to a course are to be expected, whether accompanied by diagnosis or not, given the wide cognitive diversity of students.
- We assume students are non-disabled unless we know otherwise, cementing the fiction that disability is a fringe experience rather than a common one. A neurodiversity paradigm would encourage us to proactively ask about students' access needs.
- We cut and paste legalistic and cold disability statements into our syllabi, offloading the management of disability onto another office. The neurodiversity paradigm might encourage us to view accommodations as more about teaching and relationships than compliance.

When I shared this section of the chapter with one colleague, they remarked that some of these common beliefs and behaviors are clearly problematic, but they are complex to respond to. For example, perhaps we shouldn't assume students are non-disabled, but we shouldn't assume that they are disabled either! Many of us would love to discard the legalistic and cold disability statements in our syllabi, but we are required to have them. Furthermore, while we may wish the provision of accommodations could be more relational and less compliance-based, disability services offices are also important strategic partners in supporting students. My overwhelming experience of working with faculty on inclusion issues is that instructors are very interested in including more students in their teaching, and motivated to do it, but they are also keenly aware of the barriers that they themselves face in these efforts.

As we ask how exclusionary structures can best be addressed from the standpoint of neurodiversity, we start to recognize that the complexity and diversity of neurodivergent experiences make simple solutions or corrections to these structures elusive. We may want to reevaluate our role as controlling professionals or "upholders of normality," but there may not be an obvious or best way to do this. I contend that our growing neurodiversity literacy can help us not only question exclusionary structures in higher education but also develop a nuanced analysis of some of the alternatives. As we will see in the next section, some changes that may seem at first to lower barriers introduce new ones, and some that may initially seem like superficial Band-Aids may have less obvious benefits.

There is probably no greater resource on the way higher education is structured to exclude disability than *Academic Ableism* by Jay Dolmage.[8] This chapter and book as a whole make reference to some of the core arguments from *Academic Ableism*, but it is worth reading in full for anyone interested in the themes of this book. Both the print version and the audiobook are free and open access, in a display of extraordinary commitment to accessibility on the part of the author and publisher. Dolmage's central argument is that higher education in North America is hostile to disabled people, and is constructed specifically to prevent disabled people from participating and to stigmatize, remove, or take advantage of them when they do take part.

Throughout the book, Dolmage uses various metaphors to describe academia's stance toward disability. The first is "steep steps," or extraordinary barriers to access that are accepted features of academia.[9] These can be physical (literal steps or another physical barrier to access) that are difficult for someone with a physical disability to use, and they can also be metaphorical—the exclusionary features of admissions, financial aid, and assessment we mentioned earlier in the chapter could be considered steep steps. The second metaphor is that of the retrofit: attempts to acknowledge or accommodate disability that are fundamentally afterthoughts. Physical barriers with literal steep steps may be retrofitted with ramps, and academic barriers may be addressed through accommodations but only after students disclose their disability. Universal Design, which we began discussing in chapter 3, is the final metaphor. For Dolmage, this represents the possibility of a higher education that does not ignore or outright exclude students with disabilities, and importantly, his view of Universal Design involves a transition from an architectural framework that creates access for physically disabled people to one that offers multiple dimensions of access.

In the next section, we will build our neurodiversity literacy by considering how the metaphors of steep steps, retrofits, and Universal Design interact with the neurodiversity paradigm, and how we may bring a neurodiversity perspective to bear on areas of academic life that currently assume a single correct approach.

Steep Steps

Neurodivergent people are met with steep steps everywhere they turn in their journey through higher education. Take the admissions process as an example. The system of admissions to both undergraduate and graduate programs is typically understood to be based on the idea of merit—that there are clearly definable criteria that make a person qualified to attend an institution or a particular program within it. For applicants to an academic program, these expectations likely include some combination of grades and test scores with less concrete factors such as personal statements, letters of recommendation, and various other qualities. In her book *Inside Graduate Admissions: Merit, Diversity, and Faculty Gatekeeping*, sociologist Julie R. Posselt describes the way that faculty on an admissions committee for a selective graduate program hope to evaluate potential applicants based on their likelihood of success in the program.[10] However, this likelihood is too often equated with a history of past academic success in the form of high grades or graduation from a selective institution. As Posselt sharply observes, "assuming the most accomplished applicants are the best candidates reduces doctoral education from a developmental process to a scholarly finishing school, and implies that mentoring relationships and learning environments matter little to students' success."[11] While all students must in reality go through such a developmental process, neurodivergent students in particular will probably require additional support, potentially including accommodations. It is easy to see why some students fear they could be judged unfavorably if they disclose a disability, or that at the very least their application will be tainted by the disclosure.[12] No wonder neurodivergent students often choose community colleges and other open enrollment institutions. According to one study, up to 81 percent of Autistic students participating in higher education in the United States are enrolled in community colleges.[13]

Even after neurodivergent students enter and begin to move through higher education institutions, steep steps continue to impede them. Academic conduct and integrity policies may make certain assumptions about which behaviors are normal and which merit suspicion of cheating. Neurodivergent students may also have complicated relationships with these policies because of accommodations that non-disabled students are not permitted—their accommodations would be considered cheating in another context. A neurodivergent student who is approved to have additional time would be perceived to be cheating if they used more time than their peers without disclosing their disability. This is just one example among many of how the steepest steps for neurodivergent students are those associated with assessment and grading.

Assessment, Grades, and Neurodiversity

In their book *Grading for Growth,* David Clark and Robert Talbert describe how our current grading system didn't always exist but evolved in response to increasing school and college enrollments (and the movement of students between schools) as well as the popularity of measurement instruments such as IQ tests.[14] This influence has led to assessment primarily being a practice of ranking and separating students based on their academic abilities. Where assessment could ideally be about providing instructors and students with the feedback they need to guide teaching and learning, it often ends up being little more than a sorting system. This creates a form of steep steps for educators themselves. As a faculty developer and teacher, I don't think I will ever go so far as to say that we should not assess our students' learning. However, as Neera R. Jain puts it, the project of creating an "inclusive" approach to assessment is something of a paradox because of the history of assessment as a system to sort students by ability and achievement.[15]

There is an exciting emerging literature both critiquing traditional grading systems and offering alternatives—some of which have gained significant popularity in recent years. While there have probably been instructors rejecting traditional numerical or letter-scale grading for some time, specifications, contract, and standards-based grading are just some of the approaches to emerge recently that diverge from traditional grading. Contract and specifications grading replace the subjective judgment of the assessor with a shared agreement between the instructor and the student about how work will be evaluated, what success looks like, and which activities or products are optional and which are required. Collaborative grading is another approach "in which students and instructors determine grades for a given course in consultation with one another."[16] The terms "ungrading" and "alternative grading" have emerged to describe these varied practices. The former was popularized by educator and writer Jesse Stommel, and also through online communities like Twitter and as a result of an essay collection on ungrading.[17] An umbrella term (much like "neurodiversity"), "ungrading" refers to a number of assessment and grading approaches which share a rejection of the most punitive aspects of traditional grading.

Grading is an excellent place to apply a neurodiversity analysis because the traditional methods are already so aligned with the pathology paradigm. Established approaches often define success based on a narrow set of criteria, offering little tolerance for error, and labeling students as failures if their skills and abilities do not meet these criteria. Traditional grading is associated with normality (sometimes literally in the case of curved classes), so we might expect alternative methods to be closer to a neurodiversity perspective and generally more inclusive of students with disabilities. Many alternative grading methods make fewer assumptions about the ideal way for students to express and demonstrate their knowledge, and place more focus on student autonomy and agency and an interactive feedback process. Alternative approaches also tend to value and embrace students' individual strengths and unique abilities, rather than judging only whether they do or do not match a predetermined ideal. These are all elements that mesh well with the concept of neurodiversity.

The other side of the coin, however, is that neurodiverse students and instructors (meaning many types of neurodivergent and neurotypical people) are likely to encounter friction with any grading method, whether traditional or alternative. In her book *The Hidden Inequities of Labor-Based Contract Grading*, Ellen C.

Carillo offers a sharp perspective on how simply offering an alternative to traditional grading systems does not automatically lead to equity for all students.[18] Her book is based around a simple but thought-provoking point: Replacing normative conceptions of "quality" with normative conceptions of "labor" simply reinforces a single standard of success for students, leading to new inequities.[19] The specific story here is worth delving into: Carillo's mentor Asao Inoue devised the idea of "labor-based contract grading."[20] This approach rewards students for the labor they put into writing assignments, rather than their grade being the instructor's judgment of the quality of the finished product. It might involve students agreeing to spend thirty minutes on a given assignment, with the understanding that while they will receive various types of feedback and guidance, their grade will be based on the amount of labor they put in. Inoue's purpose in developing this system was primarily to address power imbalances between writing instructors and multilingual students and students of color, whose language and writing frequently don't align with the normative expectations of the college writing classroom.

In turn, Carillo wrote her book in response to Inoue welcoming ideas to improve labor-based contract grading and address any inequities that had not been accounted for. Bringing ideas from disability studies into the conversation, she asks how students with disabilities might interact with the new grading system. Specifically, she wonders whether it relies on too normative a conception of time. Labor-based contract grading is based on the idea that each person's thirty minutes of work on a writing project should be valued equally. Citing scholars Kathleen Kryger and Griffin Zimmerman, Carillo explains that there are multiple ways in which neurodivergent students may experience time differently than neurotypical students and indeed each other.[21] Kryger and Zimmerman write,

> anxiety or depression can cause students to struggle to maintain sustained effort on a task; ADHD can

> require a student to read a passage multiple times to gain the same benefit as a neurotypical student due to difficulties in managing attention; autistic students may need assistance to produce expected levels of linguistic expression on assignments; and dyslexic students may need to access materials through differentiated technologies that require additional time investments. In each of these cases, neurodivergent students often invest more embodied/physical and emotional/affective labor toward completing the cognitive labor than a neurotypical peer but are provided the same reward for these arguably more extensive efforts.[22]

In addition to these examples, I think of the perspective that dyspraxic educator Kerry Pace shares about her own experiences in an article called "My Personal Experiences of Dyspraxia: Management Strategies and Resources for All."[23] She is a working professional in higher education and was not diagnosed as dyspraxic until the age of thirty-three. She notes that non-dyspraxic people or people who don't know about her diagnosis are very surprised by the amount of time it takes her to do things. Pace explains a key feature of her experience of neurodivergence is doing things on a different timescale than other people. It takes her longer to get dressed and leave the house, and to do other activities that involve a large number of coordinated steps.

This discussion is in no way meant to suggest that alternative grading methods should be passed over. For the majority of assignments in my own course, I favor complete/incomplete grading. This is an example of tolerance for error in assessment and involves informing a student who receives an "incomplete" grade that they have not met the expectations of the assignment and providing feedback. This is not equivalent to the negative consequences of a poor grade, as long as the student chooses to resubmit the assignment after incorporating the feedback to improve their work. Furthermore, alternative grading methods that involve students in the assessment of their own learning align with the neurodiversity paradigm and certain ideas from the neurodiversity movement: Learning does not necessarily need to take one specific form, and students themselves are a valuable source of knowledge about their learning. One potential takeaway from Carillo's work is that every approach to grading and assessment needs to be evaluated with equity in mind, even those that are designed to provide an alternative to traditional grading.

Retrofitting and Fee-Based Academic Support Programs

"Retrofitting" is Dolmage's second metaphor for how higher education interacts with disability.[24] Put most simply, retrofitting is the addition of new features to older systems that lacked those features initially. You might know the term from its architectural or construction context, in which a building or structure has features added to it years or decades after its initial construction (e.g., seismic retrofitting, in which structures are reinforced to make them more resilient to earthquakes). Retrofitting is often a response to new information or events, such as updated building codes, changing conditions like those brought on by climate change, or the availability of new technologies. In contrast, some retrofitting is done because certain users were never seriously considered among the likely or intended users of a structure.

Dolmage suggests that retrofitting often looks like a ramp on the side of a building or at the back of one. Similarly, disability as an aspect of individual experiences is often a secondary consideration in educational design. The accessible entrance "around back" is a particularly pointed example of a major issue with retrofitting: It solves the problem of disabled people's need for a way to get into the building but does so in a manner that clearly marks them as unexpected and vaguely unwelcome users of the space.

Retrofits are sometimes necessary and appropriate, but they are definitionally an afterthought or a reactive process. For example, academic accommodations are a form of retrofitting in that they provide modification after the fact to a learning experience that was designed in a particular way that was not accessible to all students. Because of their nature as afterthoughts, there are several problems with retrofits as an approach to including neurodivergent students. We will explore these through the example of fee-based academic support programs for such students.

Academic Support Programs for Neurodivergent Students

Beyond the legally mandated academic accommodations that we discussed in chapter 3, there are an ever-increasing number of what I call "fee-based academic support programs" for neurodivergent students. The programs that fall into this category cost money on top of regular tuition and other fees that are charged to students. As one example, Fairleigh Dickinson University in New Jersey offers the COMPASS program—an "individually tailored, comprehensive, academic, and social support program for a limited number of college students with Autism Spectrum Disorder."[25] At the time of writing, the program costs $3,815 per semester on top of regular tuition and fees, and offers individualized academic support for two-hours per week, individual counseling, and group therapy, as well as support in liaising with faculty. Other programs offer similar services but are not (only) focused on Autistic students. Marist University in Poughkeepsie, New York offers a learning support program for students who have received a diagnosis of a learning disability or ADHD.[26] The program offers meetings with a learning specialist as its primary benefit, as well as peer-tutoring, reading and writing assistance, and a number of other support services. It currently costs $2,850 per semester.

What makes these programs and others like them examples of retrofitting? Simply put, the services they offer are useful or necessary to some neurodivergent students' participation in college but are not offered to all students or built into a standard course of academic study. They differ notably from academic accommodations in that they cost money, while accommodations provided through a disability services office are free. The cost associated with these programs is just one example of how students who participate in them are faced with a host of extra work beyond what another student would have to do. To access many academic support programs for neurodivergent students, a student will have to:

- meet various criteria for diagnosis—this may include not just having received a valid diagnosis but within a certain period prior to applying;
- apply to the college or university and submit a second application to the support program—this may include a separate application fee, letter of recommendation, application essay, and other additional documentation not required by the institution's admissions office, like an IQ test, a psychoeducational evaluation, and copies of the student's 504 plan or Individualized Education Program from high school;
- accept an a priori agreement to participate in the program's activities, such as agreeing to meet with a tutor or coach a certain number of times per week, or enrolling in a particular support course.

If we combine the costs of these programs (which in most cases can't be paid for using federal financial aid) with the logistic hurdles to admission, it is easy to see how support programs for neurodivergent students are themselves difficult to access. This fact is somewhat ironic, given that the programs are designed to provide or augment access to education for neurodivergent students. The barriers to participation in academic support programs for students who do not (yet) have a diagnosis and those who may be unable to pay the additional fees are interrelated. Lower income students who do not yet have a diagnosis often need to pay for an evaluation in order to access even basic accommodations through a disability services office. If they receive a diagnosis and could benefit from academic support services, they may still find themselves unable to afford the program.

As discussed in chapter 3, any program or institutional approach to neurodivergent students which relies on a medical diagnosis and disclosure of that diagnosis could be understood as being part of the pathology paradigm rather than the neurodiversity paradigm. However, run thoughtfully, support programs for neurodivergent students do advance the neurodiversity paradigm on campuses. An article by higher education researcher Brett Nachman explores how an autism support program at a suburban community college affected faculty and staff perspectives on Autistic students.[27] Nachman's own position in this study is notable, as an Autistic researcher who is a community-college graduate himself. The college in his study, which is referred to by a pseudonym, has a long-established autism support program, which made it a good candidate for an exploration of its impact on attitudes among faculty and staff. Notable elements of the program that align with a neurodiversity-informed approach include having Autistic staff members working in the program and courses that focus on self-advocacy and communication. Nachman interviews a range of staff and faculty who have roles related to the support program, whether working directly in the program itself or in other jobs on the campus, such as administration. The program uses a strengths-based approach to working with Autistic students, and encourages both students and staff to approach communication difficulties with humility and a positive attitude. The director of the program "shared that autistic and neurotypical people both have a responsibility to meet each other halfway, essentially understanding their distinct ways of processing situations and sharing skills."[28]

Notably, the program that Nachman profiled in this study was not one that relied on student fees to run—it was funded by donations. Perhaps this is significant in that the program is viewed as a responsibility of the institution or community, rather than of individual students. This program provides a useful example of how a retrofit may lead to fundamental and potentially lasting changes in the approach of an institution and its staff to neurodiversity. Educators who are involved in any program designed to support neurodivergent students or provide neurodivergent students and staff with greater visibility or recognition on campus might apply a key lesson from this case study. While the structures of higher education are usually not designed with neurodivergent students in mind, initiatives for such students—and neurodivergent staff—can challenge structures and mindsets even if they use retrofits to help neurodivergent people navigate these structures.

Universal Design (for Learning)

"Universal Design" is Dolmage's third and final metaphor for the way that higher education approaches disability—or more realistically how it *could* approach disability. As part of our discussion of how the neurodiversity paradigm could be more authentically taken up in higher education, we will now explore some of the relationship between neurodiversity and UDL. While the concepts of "neurodiversity" and "UDL" come from two different sets of ideas (a social justice movement for acceptance and inclusion for Autistic people, and educational research on inclusion and disability, respectively), both offer a paradigm shift from the idea of "normality."

Let's start by reviewing the basics of UDL. It is an inclusive pedagogical framework that aims to reduce barriers in the learning environment by considering variability among learners in the design of learning. The framework emerged in the 1990s and is attributed to Harvard Graduate School of Education researchers David Rose and Anne Meyer.[29] Colloquially, UDL is often described as the practice of offering multiple options for various aspects of the learning process. The UDL guidelines which are produced and distributed by the non-profit CAST suggest that multiple options be provided for engagement (how to appeal to students' motivations and interests), representation (how information is presented and perceived), and action and expression (how students interact with materials and their peers, and demonstrate their knowledge).[30]

UDL grew out of Rose and Meyer's efforts to apply the Universal Design framework to teaching in a way that would offer disabled students greater access. The UDL framework then evolved to integrate certain findings in neuroscience into its teaching recommendations. These concern various neural networks that are involved in the learning process.[31] When UDL first emerged, "learner variability" referred to variability[32] between individuals and within the same individual with respect to how the brain processes information.[33] UDL researchers' more recent conceptions of learner variability take a more expansive perspective than only neurological differences. For example, instructional design and UDL researcher Kavita Rao has introduced a model of learner variability that includes "abilities and strengths," "support needs," "backgrounds and experiences," and "preferences and interests" as components of learner variability.[34]

I myself have been invested in the practice of UDL since I first discovered it as a graduate student. It naturally appealed to me as a student who often struggled with the prescribed way of doing things, and as an instructor who was always skeptical that I would be able to assess my students' knowledge using just one assessment method. As I became more interested in how instructors can respond to neurodiversity in the classroom, I noticed that UDL is very commonly mentioned together with neurodiversity. Sometimes, UDL is invoked as a potential teaching strategy to respond to neurodiversity, and sometimes it is more generally mentioned as a parallel or related concept.[35]

The surface-level similarity between the concepts of learner variability and neurodiversity is one potential explanation for why instructors and advocates for neurodivergent students in education believe that UDL is a useful strategy. For example, in one notable article by a group of neurodivergent students and allies titled "Building Neurodiversity-Inclusive Postsecondary

Campuses,"[36] faculty training on UDL is named as a strategy for working toward this goal—an assertion with which I agree. The assumed link between UDL and neurodiversity has always been curious to me, particularly because the two concepts have different origins. In fact, even though neurodiversity as a concept came into the public conversation in the later 1990s and early 2000s, contemporary UDL texts make no reference to it.[37]

Similarities Between UDL and Neurodiversity

Despite these non-intersecting histories, UDL and neurodiversity share an emphasis on a paradigm shift. As we know from previous chapters, neurodiversity itself is a fact about the diversity of cognition among humans, and the neurodiversity paradigm adds that this diversity is valuable and that there is no one right mind. The concept emerged out of Autistic advocacy communities that eventually became the neurodiversity movement. The concept of neurodiversity implies a paradigm shift from a pathological view of cognitive difference to one that is accepting of diversity. Similarly, UDL represents a shift from a paradigm of an average expected student to one of learner variability, which might also be termed "diversity."[38] This shared resistance to the idea that there is an obvious way to be "normal" or "average" offers an opportunity for partnership between UDL and neurodiversity. UDL's focus on learner variability also provides a useful lens for considering the variability within neurodivergence itself. As discussed in previous chapters, neurodivergence is an umbrella concept covering conditions and experiences of cognitive difference from societal norms. Neurodivergent people as a group don't have one particular set of characteristics or needs, even though some characteristics—such as executive functioning or sensory processing differences—are shared by different subgroups of neurodivergent people. Thus, even in a class made up only of neurodivergent people, UDL would still be a useful teaching framework because there is no average student to plan for.

Opportunities for Growth

Given these strong conceptual similarities, I believe UDL can be even further informed by ideas from neurodiversity, such as the lessons from the neurodiversity movement we discussed in chapter 2. While UDL considers the variability among learners to be an essential starting point for learning design, its conception of learner variability is mostly concerned with variability that clearly affects *learning*. This could be cognitive differences in how people process information, or different backgrounds or interests that affect learners' engagement. Neurodiversity as a concept and movement recognizes that cognition, behavior, and communication are all variable traits, and ignoring individual differences within all these categories can only create barriers for neurodivergent people. For example, UDL supports varied communication methods, but it might benefit from addressing communication as a right (as advocate Jordyn Zimmerman does—discussed in chapter 2). The neurodiversity movement has raised awareness about barriers to neurodivergent thriving, including stereotypes and a focus on cure rather than well-being and functioning. At the time of writing, the current UDL framework (UDL 3.0) calls on instructors and students to address their biases.[39] However, the activities of the neurodiversity movement show that the types of biases that most impact neurodivergent people are assumptions about the inherent deficits associated with different diagnoses. UDL has been critiqued for focusing too much on accessibility for all learners and moving away from its roots in disability access. Further engagement with ideas from neurodiversity could help to make sure the UDL framework maintains this important connection.

In keeping with a non-utopian (but appreciative) perspective on Universal Design, we can say that UDL has much in common with neurodiversity, and is viewed positively by advocates and instructors who are interested in neuroinclusion, but that there is still work to do to further define and critically assess UDL as a response to neurodiversity in the classroom. In short, the connection between UDL and neurodiversity is a friendship worth fostering.

Takeaways

Throughout this chapter, we have seen examples of how the pathology paradigm (or medical model of disability) is present in higher education: Teachers can act as enforcers of normality. Steep steps abound in areas such as admissions, student conduct and academic integrity policies, and grading methods. When we confront these structures, we find that potential solutions are always more complex than they initially appear. Alternative grading methods are not always accessible to neurodivergent and disabled students. Academic support programs for neurodivergent students may feel like a burdensome retrofit, but they can be a bridge to a wider embrace of the neurodiversity paradigm. UDL may feel like the perfect response to neurodiversity, but it could benefit from greater engagement with the principal lessons from the neurodiversity movement.

Teaching Invitations

- Consider ways in which you may act as a "controlling professional" in your life as an educator—these areas may benefit from more reflection and study.
- When considering retrofitted methods to support neurodivergent students and staff, consider ways to reduce the burdens or new access concerns these introduce.
    - Consider how costs, additional logistic burdens, and other "disability taxes" could be reduced or eliminated.
- Be aware of how some retrofitted methods of support may create openings for greater embrace of the neurodiversity paradigm down the road.

- Consider how neurodiversity can inform teaching practices based on learning science (e.g., UDL) without collapsing these two concepts into one.
- Treat yourself kindly and don't be too discouraged in situations where responding to exclusionary norms is an uphill battle. Inclusion is an incredibly complex process, and there is no quick fix.

5

TEACHING IN THE NEURODIVERSITY PARADIGM

So far, this book has attempted to build readers' neurodiversity literacy. We have defined and explored the history of a number of important key terms, as well as discussed how to use them in our higher education context. We have traced the history of the concept of neurodiversity from its roots in Autistic self-advocacy to its broader application today. We have noted that the neurodiversity movement has emphasized the importance of authentic relationships between neurotypical and neurodivergent people, humanizing and less pathological language and discussion of neurodivergence, and research, therapies, and supports that aim to improve quality of life and functioning. We have also discussed how neurodiversity and neurodivergence relate to the larger category of disability, and how higher education has—to put it mildly—lots of opportunities for educators to be more informed by the neurodiversity paradigm.

Now, we will turn to a crucial question: How might our growing understanding of neurodiversity as a concept, movement, and way of viewing cognitive differences affect our mindsets and behaviors as instructors? The rest of this chapter provides some potential answers. Throughout the preceding chapters, we have discussed the importance of the neurodiversity paradigm and its assertion that there is not necessarily one right way to think, behave, or communicate. Nick Walker, the Autistic psychologist and proponent of the neurodiversity paradigm, has coined another term that has had less uptake in popular discourse, but which is no less thought-provoking and inspiring: "neurocosmopolitanism." Just as a cosmopolitan attitude is one of openness and appreciation toward a variety of cultures, someone who adopts a neurocosmopolitan attitude embraces the neurodiversity paradigm, actively considering the potential value of different ways of thinking. As part of a set of provocations about what a neurocosmopolitan attitude would look like in different areas of society, Walker asks,

> What might classroom education look like at various levels from preschool through grad school, in the context of a neurocosmopolitan approach to education in which it's built into the curriculum that every person in the class, teachers and students alike, works at learning to comprehend and accommodate the neurocognitive styles and communication needs of every other person in the class as best they can? What if both the education of youth and adults, and the training of educators, included the explicit understanding that no neurocognitive style is more "correct" or "normal" than any other, and that the work of mutual accommodation is both an essential part of a proper education and an essential preparation for being a participating citizen in a civilized society?[1]

I find these provocations useful because they offer an alternative perspective on neurodiversity in education to one that asks what challenges neurodivergent students face and how to mitigate them. Instead, what if the recognition of neurodiversity and efforts toward embracing it were deeply embedded in our learning environments? One reason I named this book *Classroom Mindscapes: An Introduction to Neurodiversity for Educators* is that I wanted to take this broader perspective. While conversations about the challenges neurodivergent students face are important, the way they are conducted often crosses the line into excessively deficit-based conceptions of the students. It is frequently useful and indeed necessary to provide information about some of the things neurodivergent students struggle with and how they can be supported, but as I hope the previous chapters have shown, I believe that neurodiversity offers us a different paradigm for thinking about cognitive differences, and this applies to our own classrooms as well.

Existing Pedagogical Strategies for Supporting Neurodivergent Students

If we dig into the literature providing suggestions for teaching certain groups of neurodivergent students, we can find a number of concrete recommendations that seem simple and intuitive. I preface our discussion by summarizing some of these recommendations, even though they make a lot of perhaps unjustified assumptions about the similarity of students who fall into the various groups. A study quoted in the book *College Success for Students on the Autism Spectrum: A Neurodiversity Perspective* suggests six categories of teaching strategies that could support Autistic college students. They include:

Classroom organization (informing students of the structure of the course and each class period, listing activities in an accessible location each day, explicitly state any classroom norms or expectations);

Lesson organization (Offer reminders for what will be covered in class, create a graphic organizer of the content for that day, provide lecture notes or an outline);

Design of class materials (Keep information on PowerPoints to a minimum, simplify instructions, use bold print to highlight important points);

Visual Organizers (Use charts to organize information—e.g., compare and contrast, problem and solution);

Assessment (Give shorter and more frequent exams, use multiple question types on each exam, give students choice of assessment type);
Collaboration and Social Engagement (Use group learning, encourage information sharing on chats and blogs).[2]

This is a concise and potentially useful set of ideas, though it certainly raises some new questions. If we know that Autistic students often encounter challenges with communication and social interactions, to what end should we use group-based learning? Is it important to frame information in binary ways even if we don't feel like that is the most useful approach in our own subject area? Should we deduce from the suggestions to limit information on PowerPoints and provide graphic organizers that Autistic students are less successful with printed text? This is not a challenge for Autistic college students that the authors note, though they do describe challenges with organization, handling extraneous information and sensory input, and the "ability to communicate succinctly, sequence spoken and written answers, engage in discourse, and ask/answer questions."[3] Even if the authors are correct that these are common challenges for Autistic students, they may not apply to all of this group.

I also observe that some of the challenges listed have somewhat easily available "solutions" (organization is a challenge, so offer lecture notes or a graphic organizer), but others do not have such simple answers. These are often the relational or communication challenges: There is no readily available solution to students' challenges with succinct communication, turn-taking, and contributing to a larger discourse[4] because this would likely involve the cooperation of other members of the learning community. Perhaps the instructor could provide support such as clear guidelines for a class discussion or time to compose answers ahead of the discussion, but other students would also need to be respectful or at least tolerant of their peers' different communication styles. We could undoubtedly imagine many ways to help other students develop this attitude, but they don't seem to be reflected in these recommendations.

I am ultimately in favor of any strategies available to support any individual or group of neurodivergent students. What I find lacking in the current conversation about supporting such students is any response to the neurodiversity paradigm, at least in its fullest expression. What I mean by this is that these approaches to support often still label students as deficient in some way. They all are also very focused on neurodivergent students themselves, as a potential challenge to overcome or navigate, while placing relatively little collective responsibility on teachers, students, and to a certain extent administrators to develop a mutual understanding. The last shortcoming of the available approaches is their characterization of neurodivergent students as the sole group of concern, when the reality is that neurodivergent staff and faculty are also part of the neurodiversity of a given campus, department, or classroom.

In contrast, I propose that neurodiversity can inform our teaching through an idea I call **teaching in the neurodiversity paradigm**. Recall that the neurodiversity paradigm introduced by Walker is a set of assumptions about neurodiversity that can help us to see cognitive diversity as valuable, and to invest in structures and practices that embrace neurodiversity. As mentioned at the start of this chapter, we may ultimately draw on another of Walker's ideas and aim to adopt an attitude of neurocosmopolitanism.

Walker writes, "Neurocosmopolitanism consists of approaching neurodiversity in the same spirit in which the cosmopolite approaches cultural diversity. To embrace the neurodiversity paradigm is to refuse to pathologize neurocognitive styles and experiences that differ from our own, and to accept neurodiversity as a natural, healthy, and important form of human biodiversity—a fundamental and vital characteristic of the human species, a crucial source of evolutionary and creative potential."[5]

Teaching in the neurodiversity paradigm, then, involves finding how we might take these ideas into account in our teaching.

I am very wary of introducing a brand-new Teaching Framework with a capital "T" and "F" in this book. Therefore, I will explicitly say that the ideas in this chapter do not constitute a teaching approach per se. Instead, they provide a lens through which we can consider existing teaching approaches. In keeping with neurodiversity's emphasis on multiplicity and the idea that there is no one right way to think, behave or communicate, I suggest that there is no single correct "neurodiversity-informed" teaching approach either. Rather, the teaching approaches or frameworks that we already use (e.g., UDL, project-based or team-based learning, active learning, digital pedagogy) could benefit from analysis based on neurodiversity. This may seem like a fine distinction, but I think viewing neurodiversity as a holistic consideration for teaching—rather than only thinking in terms of tips and strategies for teaching neurodivergent students—is something that most educators can benefit from, no matter how they like to teach. Even though shifting to the neurodiversity paradigm will likely require us to redefine our terms and reconsider many assumptions, this does not necessarily mean we need to completely discard teaching approaches that work for us. Teaching in the neurodiversity paradigm does represent a paradigm shift, but it is hopefully one that prompts a careful analysis of your existing teaching, rather than one that makes you feel like you are starting from square one.

Universal Design as a Place to Start

If you are familiar with either inclusive teaching approaches or have some interest in the experiences of students with disabilities in higher education, you have likely encountered UDL, which was discussed in chapter 4. It is relatively easy to find examples of UDL being invoked as a suitable response to neurodiversity in higher education. For example, the websites of multiple centers for teaching and learning throughout the United States have pages that suggest UDL as a possible teaching approach to respond to neurodiversity in the classroom. While on the surface UDL does seem to draw on some of the same themes as neurodiversity (variability, not expecting an average learner), we saw in chapter 4 how UDL is a potential ally concept to neurodiversity but not deeply informed by it.

Overall, UDL has only been taken up modestly in higher education. Several researchers and practitioners have noted how the three basic principles of UDL are beneficial for moving toward greater accessibility, even though the more specific UDL guidelines may be less so. One of the most notable scholars in this area is Jay Dolmage, whose writing on Universal Design in education has shaped much of my own thinking. In an article in *Disability Studies Quarterly,* Dolmage argues for a more critical application of UDL in teaching, suggesting that multiple means of engagement, representation, and action and expression are "places to start" rather than the sum total of Universal Design.[6] Indeed, there are other understandings of what Universal Design might mean in higher education. Notable examples are the frameworks of Universal Design for Instruction and Universal Instructional Design, developed at the University of Washington and University of Connecticut respectively. These frameworks differ from UDL in two ways: They were developed specifically with higher education contexts in mind (while UDL was originally conceived for the K–12 context), and they adhere more closely to the seven principles of Universal Design, which focus on access to learning rather than learning outcomes.

What are the drawbacks when Universal Design is treated as a destination, rather than a journey or simply a place to start? One tension that emerges is that certain applications of Universal Design sometimes function to limit discussion of disability or even conversations about student needs more generally, rather than leading to greater engagement. Dolmage refers to this phenomenon as a "defeat device."[7] The concept of a defeat device is based on Volkswagen's response to the fact that its cars that did not comply with emissions requirements. The company created a device that could temporarily make it seem as if its cars' emissions were less than they were (although the true emissions remained unchanged). The entire and only purpose of the device was to meet or get around the requirements, without actually addressing the concern that the cars' emissions were above the set levels. Dolmage shares the following anecdote to help illustrate defeat devices:

> A colleague recently posted on social media that disabled students had come to them with institutional accommodation forms, but said "Actually, the way you've designed this course, there's nothing I need changed to accommodate me." Ostensibly, they had seen the syllabus and decided that the class was going to meet their needs. It sounds like a nice, feel-good story. But it actually may be evidence of the syllabus as a defeat device.[8]

This stopped me in my tracks the first time I read it, as I had never thought of an account such as this as anything other than a "feel-good story." Dolmage suggests that though it is commendable to design a course so it limits the need for accommodations, attempting to officially certify the lack of this need after a review of the syllabus implies that both the needs of the student with a disability and the way the course will unfold are *fixed*. This is obviously very far from the truth. Just as the defeat device inside the Volkswagen car only serves to avoid the scrutiny of emissions testers, a syllabus designed to avoid the need for accommodations ignores the underlying purpose of accommodations (to facilitate access to education). It is because of the phenomenon of the defeat device that I now prefer to think of Universal Design and its application in teaching as less about avoiding the need for accommodations and more about being open to diverse needs and committed to addressing them.

As we position UDL as a place to start for teaching that affirms neurodiversity and aligns with the neurodiversity paradigm, it is useful to underscore three points.

1. UDL—the framework offered by CAST—is only one way to implement the broader concept of Universal Design in educational contexts. Applying other Universal Design ideas, such as the principle of *tolerance for error*, may be useful in responding to neurodiversity in educational contexts.
2. In its current form, UDL is not yet particularly informed by neurodiversity (the concept and movement).
3. Several ideas from the UDL framework are compatible with and can be enhanced by ideas relating to neurodiversity. These include the assumption of learner variability in learning design, honoring multiple forms of communication, and centering learner agency (see chapter 4 for a longer discussion).

A Lens: Teaching in the Neurodiversity Paradigm

If Universal Design is a "place to start" or, as Margaret Price calls it, a "way to move"[9] then the questions that follow for our approach to neurodiversity-informed teaching are clearly "Where should we go next?" and "What moves should we make?" As already mentioned, I propose the idea of teaching in the neurodiversity paradigm. This is an approach that builds on Universal Design and integrates several ideas that derive specifically from the neurodiversity conversation, highlighting the frictions and negotiations that become inevitable when we embrace neurodiversity in the classroom. I frame teaching in the neurodiversity paradigm as a practice of navigating and negotiating multiple, sometimes contrasting needs among students and teachers.

Even though my perspective on neurodiversity and teaching has always been influenced by the neurodiversity paradigm, the reason that I began to label my approach "teaching in the neurodiversity paradigm"—rather than "teaching neurodivergent students" or "supporting neurodivergent learners"—was because I felt it was strange to discuss my approach using those terms when I, the instructor, am also neurodivergent. In fact, I have gone through a fair number of courses where I was, to my knowledge, the only neurodivergent person in the classroom (student or instructor). If you have made it this far in the book, you might be thinking that this is not very likely, but both these points together are important: Teaching in a way that takes neurodiversity seriously shouldn't be only about students, and it shouldn't depend on someone disclosing a diagnosis or identity.

Teaching in the neurodiversity paradigm is a way of bringing an appreciation and understanding of neurodiversity to our teaching that not only supports neurodivergent students and instructors, but also considers the benefits of a neurodiversity perspective for everyone in the learning community, especially as a way to navigate multiple different and potentially contrasting needs. As Ash Lierman notes in their book *The Struggle You Can't See: Experiences of Neurodivergent and Invisibly Disabled Students in Higher Education*, many students with disabilities (including many neurodivergent students) choose not to disclose their disability "either because they anticipate stigma, they have internalized stigma, or in many cases, because they have actually experienced stigma in the past."[10] Adopting the neurodiversity paradigm more fully in our teaching could also help some students consider or accept their own neurodivergence in ways that they might not have been willing or able to do previously.

There are three main components to this lens, which I will explain one by one:

1. the neurodiversity paradigm
2. tolerance for error
3. access friction

The Neurodiversity Paradigm

When we consider the neurodiversity paradigm in teaching, we recognize that cognitive differences do not need to be seen as problems by default. To review, the paradigm has three components, which we will unpack individually from the perspective of an instructor. Paraphrasing Walker's initial description of the neurodiversity paradigm, these are as follows:

1. The cognitive diversity among humans is natural and valuable.
2. There is no one right way to think, behave, or communicate, any more than there is one right race, gender, or ethnicity.
3. There can be harmful expressions of power and control but also major opportunities for flourishing when diversity is embraced.

COGNITIVE DIVERSITY AMONG HUMANS IS NATURAL AND VALUABLE

On the face of it, this statement seems easy to accept. From an instructor's or student's point of view, who would want a classroom with only one type of person, style of thought, or perspective? I tingle with excitement when I read my students' introductions at the beginning of semester, taking in the wide range of life experiences and interests within the class. But underlying this first component of the neurodiversity paradigm is also the diversity of cognition that produces disability in our society as it is currently organized: differences in perception, language, the senses, and processing speeds that are labeled as dyslexia, learning disabilities, and sensory processing disabilities among others. A teacher who took this principle of the neurodiversity paradigm seriously would need to reconsider whether these disabilities are by default pathologies or deficits. Indeed, as we discussed in chapter 1, many neurodivergent people have particular strengths that exist alongside some of their challenges.

However expected and potentially valuable cognitive diversity may be in a learning situation, instructors may find embracing it a challenge when it complicates their own plans or goals in the classroom. When I was meeting a group of instructors in the television and media field, one of them told me that he incorporated role-playing activities into his course to provide students with opportunities to practice working in the small teams that produce and edit television content. One neurodivergent student, Cole, insisted that he did not want to participate in the role-playing activity. Cole said he didn't understand the purpose of "pretending" to be in a certain role, rather than having the teacher explain to him the tasks and skills necessary for it. He refused to take part, requesting an alternative option. The teacher expressed significant frustration. According to him, the role-playing activities were self-evidently useful, and Cole didn't seem to recognize his own unreasonable bias against them.

We can use this story to consider how challenging it may be to embrace the first principle of the neurodiversity paradigm. Based on our view that cognitive diversity among humans is natural and valuable, we might need to reframe the situation: Rather than a source of frustration for the instructor, Cole's perspective could be seen as representing a different way of thinking about learning and collaboration. But what would it look like to view this student's different perspective as a positive? In all likelihood, it would require us to reconsider the assumption that role-playing activities are self-evidently beneficial. Even if they are beneficial and enjoyable for many or even most students, perhaps they are not for *all*. Those students who do not see the activities as self-evidently useful might come to see their value after additional explanation and discussion. But some might not.

What is the potential value of these differences? At the very least, Cole's resistance to the role-playing might have had the benefit of prompting the instructor to consider and then clarify the activity's goals. Thinking more expansively, there may be a certain value in a reluctance to act a role that one isn't very well prepared for. The conceit of role-playing activities in a classroom is that the learning environment is a low-stakes space, where one can make mistakes and learn from them. However, Cole may be drawing on a range of experiences and ways of thinking that lead him to believe that there are risks to jumping into a role that he does not feel well prepared for. If the stakes in a situation are sufficiently high and there are more experienced or qualified people around, it does not make sense to "build the plane while you fly it."

Another possibility is that Cole found it difficult to buy into the fiction that the group was in a real television production situation. While I do not know if this student was Autistic, he demonstrated a common Autistic way of thinking that has been observed in research: He was more reluctant than other students to put aside the "truth" that this was not a real television studio and act the role he was assigned. This is not to say that the student would not have been successful in acting that role if he felt that participating was worthwhile. As an aside, Autistic people can be quite good at playing acting roles in many situations, and a number of well-known actors are Autistic.

This anecdote illustrates how the first principle of the neurodiversity paradigm may be difficult to embrace when cognitive diversity creates friction in the classroom, as it did in this scenario. The student's different way of thinking about the idea of the role-playing activity may have caused friction in several ways. The instructor hadn't anticipated that students might object to or not understand the exercise, so this interrupted the planned agenda for the session. The instructor had likewise not planned an alternative activity that this student might do, given his reluctance to role-play. Accepting that cognitive variation is at least potentially valuable is especially difficult under the stresses of week-to-week teaching. Sometimes, it is helpful to name this challenge rather than ignore it. If I find myself getting frustrated, I always find it helpful to explain to a student that my frustration is a lot more about external constraints like time and resource availability than about them.

This first principle of the neurodiversity paradigm also provides scope to encourage students to remain open to learning activities that are not ideal for them. I often remind my students or participants in faculty development programs that I know every activity will not align perfectly with their learning needs or preferences, but that they might be able to see the value of an activity through analogy. If I were the instructor in this story, I might ask Cole if he could see any benefits of role-playing activities in general. Has there ever been a situation in which he learned something important through role-play, and could some of the same benefits apply here? Reframing role-playing as a skill to develop (rather than an easy way to learn something) might also help Cole here if his resistance is partly because the dynamics of the role-playing activity feel overwhelming to him. When I was a student, I was much more open to attempting learning activities when the instructor acknowledged that they might take some time to get used to, rather than assuming their usefulness was immediately and intuitively obvious to all.

THERE IS NO ONE RIGHT WAY TO THINK, BEHAVE, OR COMMUNICATE

Teaching in the neurodiversity paradigm will require us to be curious in our approach to misunderstandings and communication difficulties. In chapter 2, I introduced scholarship by the Autistic researcher Damian Milton who has sought to revise a stereotype about Autistic people that pervades the fields of psychology and psychiatry as well as wider society: that Autistics struggle with interpersonal communication and understanding other people's intentions or perspectives. This generalization is so pervasive that people often can easily give examples from popular media in which a character is coded as Autistic or otherwise neurodivergent simply because they experience confusion about social cues (examples from TV shows that come to my mind are Abed from *Community* and Dwight from *The Office*). Milton suggests that this generalization is unnecessarily one-sided—the Autistic person lacks empathy for the non-Autistic person. Then, questioning whether the communication difficulties between two people are, by definition, one person's fault, Milton proposes the "double empathy" perspective: It is not just that Autistic people sometimes struggle to communicate with non-Autistic people, but also that non-Autistic people struggle to communicate with Autistic people.[11]

APPLYING DOUBLE EMPATHY IN THE CLASSROOM

For our purposes, let's extend the concept of double empathy beyond the categories of Autistic and non-Autistic to say that people in general are not guaranteed to understand each other and communicate effectively without laying some groundwork first. We might further say that effective communication is unlikely to develop without goodwill and a willingness to try on both sides. As introductory communication courses tend to say, there is no communication that only involves one person. I certainly don't mean for this generalization of double empathy to gloss over the way that neurodivergent people are often blamed for interpersonal conflicts and misunderstandings. Instead, to illustrate how this framework might be helpful, I will provide some anecdotes from higher ed contexts that I think exemplify how double empathy can inform our thinking about truly shared and collective responsibility and investment in developing mutual understanding.

The critical element of my extension of double empathy is that misunderstandings and communication difficulties don't inherently need to be seen as one party's fault, as long as the people involved are putting effort into resolving any misunderstanding. The idea that one person or group is solely responsible for difficulties in communicating could be regarded as aligning with the pathology paradigm. This view would suggest that in addition to there being a right type of mind, there is a right style of communication. If we apply the neurodiversity paradigm and consider that there isn't any absolutely right way to communicate, we may be able to leave behind any view of communication problems as adversarial conflicts and perceive them more neutrally. I myself always find it easier to resolve a conflict if I and the other person can agree that neither person is at fault.

One small change in line with this idea has helped me a lot as an instructor. I expect many other instructors have had students ask questions in response to course information along the lines of "Can I submit assignments late?" or "What should we submit for the final project?" My reaction to these types of questions always used to be one of two extremes: blaming myself entirely or blaming the student entirely. When blaming myself, I would think, "My whole job as a teacher is to make all the information completely clear and accessible to students, and I failed." When blaming the student, I would think, "The syllabus very clearly says that I will accept late assignments and that they should submit a five-page paper or ten-minute video for the project. Why can't they just read that information?" When I have tried applying the insights of double empathy, I have realized that engaging with such questions in a way that avoids blame means I learn more about what is behind the question and what information students actually need.

As discussed later, in the section on *tolerance for error* in teaching, there are many different reasons why expectations may seem clear to one person but not to another. When a student asked me last semester whether they could submit assignments late, I learned from the subsequent conversation that they were skeptical about the information I had provided because they had never had an instructor who allowed students to submit work late with no penalty. I explained that instructors have a certain amount of autonomy in how they run their classrooms—a component of the larger concept of "academic freedom." The communication difficulty here was not because I hadn't ever stated my approach to late work, or even because the student hadn't read this statement, but because the student lacked important context to help them decide what to do with the information I had provided. I believe that approaching this conflict without attempting to assign blame helped us both learn something useful.

My extension of double empathy could also be helpful for neurodivergent people when they are working with a neurotypical person who has expressed interest in being their ally but has difficulty taking the neurodivergent person's perspective. One higher ed staff member I spoke with told me about a neurodivergent student—we can call her Tamara—who had gone through a great deal of exclusion and rejection in her previous social and educational experiences, which Tamara attributed to her different communication style, affect, and social style. Tamara felt it was a good idea to disclose her neurodivergence to instructors, so they could understand a particular aspect of her learning needs: She found it almost impossible to embark on any activity or assignment until she felt that she perfectly understood all of the instructions. This was because of her past experiences of misinterpreting or misjudging expectations.

In many instances, individual instructors and disability services staff were willing and able to support Tamara's needs and used strategies like scheduling meetings or sending emails that would help to clarify instructions and expectations. Several of Tamara's instructors were knowledgeable about neurodivergence and expressed their allyship to her. However, two additional factors meant Tamara's situation came to a head in an upper-level philosophy class taught by an instructor named Denzil. One was that her anxiety about misjudging expectations did not seem to reduce even after repeated good faith attempts to clarify them, supported by both instructors and disability services staff. The other was that Tamara found it difficult to receive any feedback at all—whether negative or constructive—because she suspected that it was really evidence of her instructor's bias against her neurotype. Tamara was convinced that Denzil fundamentally couldn't understand her neurodivergent communication style, and her relationship with the instructor broke down. Denzil felt that he was being supportive and accommodating but that he was still obligated to provide the kind of constructive feedback that would help Tamara improve her work.

When I was asked for advice on how Tamara, Denzil, and the colleague who told me this story could move forward, I first wondered whether there were any course design changes (in this case to be applied retroactively) that could have helped to ease the tension. As discussed in chapter 4, there might also be an opportunity to use some lower-stakes approaches to assessment and grading to make sure that communication differences didn't feel like such crises to the student because of grade anxiety.

I also thought immediately of double empathy and how it might be useful in this situation, for all parties. Applying our extension of double empathy that says we need not assign blame when communication between two people is difficult, I might ask Tamara whether we can acknowledge that establishing mutual understanding has indeed been difficult in this situation without characterizing Denzil as being responsible for this. In all cases, we must remember that the concept of double empathy doesn't simply aim to shift the blame for communication difficulties so that it resides with the neurotypical person rather than the neurodivergent person. While it is quite possible that this communication difficulty occurred simply because of the parties' different ways of thinking, it would not be unreasonable for Tamara to give Denzil more credit for his efforts.

THERE CAN BE HARMFUL EXPRESSIONS OF POWER AND CONTROL BUT ALSO MAJOR OPPORTUNITIES FOR FLOURISHING WHEN DIVERSITY IS EMBRACED

Power is not evenly distributed among the different people who participate in higher education, to say the least. Teaching in the neurodiversity paradigm can help us surface power imbalances so that we may work toward embracing neurodiversity rather than reinforcing harmful hierarchies of cognitive and behavioral traits. For example, it is easy to view communication differences in terms of "good communicators" and "bad communicators" because communication norms are very strong in our society. In line with our discussion of the previous principle, let us accept that differences in communication do not automatically mean that one way is better and one way is worse. Another way of saying this is that everyone has strengths and challenges in how they communicate, and whether a specific trait is a strength or challenge is likely to depend on context. A simple example is that my speaking voice is naturally very quiet, with the upper level of my volume range being what most people would use to talk to their companion in a moderately busy restaurant. This particular trait is useful for communication in libraries or other quiet spaces and for talking to people who are sensitive to sound. It is not advantageous for teaching or presenting to large groups or talking to a relative who is partially deaf. I feel very lucky that people who find it difficult to hear me don't write me off as a poor communicator or decide that it isn't worth working out a way to understand me.

Here is a different example related to a learning situation that one of my colleagues described to me. In a political science class she was teaching, this colleague assigned students to go in small groups to different locations on campus and poll passersby on their opinions on a political issue. The first telling of the story demonstrates how power imbalances and hierarchy can limit the potential benefits of neurodiversity and exclude neurodivergent people. The second version shows how embracing neurodiversity can make it a source of potential and flourishing.

Version 1: *The instructor, who we will call Tiana, speaks to each group before they set out to do their polling. She tells the members of one group that they are going to a busy area of a library and will have to figure out a way to stop a certain number of people and poll them, as this activity is designed to be completed during a single class period. Tiana adds that the students should select "someone who is a good communicator, a people person with an engaging personality" to approach potential participants and conduct the conversation with them, as people are more likely to stop and volunteer their time for someone charismatic. She says that the other members of the group* *can record responses or think about how they want to present their data to the rest of the class when they return. One student in this group, Troy, has dyspraxia. His condition involves difficulty with motor planning. Spontaneous speech and reading printed material out loud can be challenging for him. His fellow students don't know his diagnosis but do know that these activities are hard for him, and that most people perceive him as neurodivergent. On the walk over to the location where they will conduct their poll, a talkative and confident student named Marc volunteers to "do the talking."*

Version 2: *Tiana briefs the groups before they leave the classroom to begin their polling. She says that to execute the activity, one student will need to attract the attention of busy students and faculty who are passing by the location and tell them that the group is taking a poll. Then, another student will need to read them a script and get their answer to the poll question, and a further student will record their responses. As a result of his dyspraxia, Troy has much more success with spontaneous, short verbal communications—like greetings—than planning and speaking longer sentences. This strength of Troy's communication could make him well suited to the task of getting potential participants' attention by saying, "Hi, good morning!" and waving, which he volunteers to do. Another student who is a fast typist volunteers to record the conversations. Marc decides to read the question to the participants.*

While Tiana's approach in the second version of this scenario doesn't guarantee that Troy won't be excluded, it at least establishes that she views the assignment as being about something more complex than "good communication." She acknowledges that different types of communication can contribute to the group, so no one participant emerges as its sole voice.

Tolerance for Error

In chapter 3, we discussed tolerance for error as an aspect of Universal Design that could support neurodivergent students.

Tolerance for error is an important component of teaching in the neurodiversity paradigm because it helps instructors ensure that differences in communication and understanding do not have adverse consequences for learners. As discussed in chapters 3 and 4, this final principle can be viewed as aligning with the neurodiversity paradigm because it creates space for multiple ways to be right or fewer ways to be wrong. Tolerance for error in teaching could also mean reducing the stakes of misunderstanding or mistakes when there actually is a specific requirement or expectation. The way I have attempted to operationalize this in my own teaching, and how I sometimes advise others to do so, is to consider one's own instructional design and teaching behaviors as parts of a *process* of building understanding between the instructor and students, and between the students themselves. Perfect understanding is not a realistic goal from the moment an assignment is distributed.

I think this is true, even though the practice of giving advance clarification of expectations as part of assignment instructions is popular and supported by research. If you have been plugged into the pedagogical research and educational development worlds for a while, you might hear the phrase "make expectations explicit" and think of the Transparency in Learning and Teaching (TILT) framework.[12] I knew of and used the TILT framework before I started working seriously with neurodiversity in teaching, in part because its theory and research base suggested that it benefited first-generation students. I am not a first-generation student, but I struggled quite a bit with understanding the expectations of my instructors throughout my undergraduate and graduate programs. Even though lack of clarity about expectations and goals may disproportionately affect certain groups of students (perhaps neurodivergent, first-generation, or international students, to name a few), I imagine many people have their own story from their higher ed experience that made them feel like Amelia Bedelia—the children's book character who misinterprets norms and instructions with hilarious and often embarrassing results.

I recall a student who brought athletic clothing and sneakers to class because it was described as taking place in an "active learning classroom."

Ever the one to intensively analyze children's books, I was always very annoyed by the fact that the "joke" in each Amelia Bedelia book is that Amelia messes up the instructions for each new occupation she tries (office clerk, teacher, babysitter) even though she has never done those jobs before. Success at any job relies on specialized knowledge, likely developed over time. On a deep dive into this book series, I discovered a widespread fan theory that Amelia Bedelia is Autistic or neurodivergent, presumably based on the idea that Autistic people tend to interpret information in a literal way. I think there is even a deeper lesson in these stories about how people think and communicate: Some of the misunderstandings between Amelia Bedelia and her boss Mrs. Rogers might have been unavoidable even with maximum effort in making expectations explicit. In one instance, Mrs. Rogers asks Amelia to "remove some spots" from a dress, by which she means use a stain-removing cleaning product, but which Amelia interprets as an instruction to cut the spots out of the dress with scissors.[13] It took me a couple of minutes to break down this particular misunderstanding and put into words how each character is interpreting the directions, a process which is much easier *after* the misunderstanding has played out. In short, potential misunderstandings of expectations are hard to identify in advance, and people don't always accurately predict how others will interpret what they say. I have come to the conclusion that "making your expectations explicit" seems like a very easy thing to do, but it can be quite difficult in reality. This is why tolerance for error is needed in so many teaching situations.

Much of the frustration I experience in teaching, and in life more generally, comes from having painstakingly written out or otherwise communicated instructions as clearly as I can, only to have a student, fellow community member, or even my two-year-old interpret them differently or tell me that I have not been clear.

From the perspective of the neurodiversity paradigm, no one has done anything wrong when one person feels they have made their expectations explicit and another person simply . . . doesn't understand them. For example, students' perceptions of expectations may be influenced by information other than what you yourself provide. On one occasion, I was corresponding with a student about the expectations for a discussion board assignment. I had indicated that I didn't expect students to use a formal, "research paper"-style tone for the posts, but that they should use a specific referencing format if they cited any sources. I reminded the student of this in my feedback on a post, and they responded that they had assumed that the formal style was necessary because one of their other instructors had encouraged it. The college where I teach the course in question does have a number of policies to standardize certain elements of the student academic experience (common syllabus templates, course shells, weekly course rhythms, etc.) so this wasn't an unreasonable inference.

In this situation, I hadn't failed to communicate my expectations; it was just that my student's perception of them had been affected by other information beyond the instructions I had given. In a Zoom class session for the same course, students took a certain action to mark themselves present for the class, despite the fact that I had never asked them to do so. Again, it was a requirement of another professor that they assumed I shared (even though I was totally unaware of it). Tolerance for error here is not so hard to activate because it requires very little of me to clarify the misunderstanding. If we approach these events with curiosity, many of them can be wonderful learning opportunities about what is going on in our students' minds.

As exemplified in the earlier anecdote about neurodivergent student Tamara and her instructor Denzil, questions about clarifying instructions and the expectations for class assignments can be more charged matters in student-instructor interactions that involve neurodivergence. In those interactions, tolerance for error may feel harder for instructors—and students—to access, but in

Tamara's case, the principle might have been applied by attempting to reduce her anxiety about her communication and comprehension differences by offering her a guaranteed opportunity to redo assignments after feedback.

One question you might have is: "Doesn't this concept of tolerance for error have some similarities with retrofitting?" As discussed in chapter 4, retrofitting is the metaphor that Dolmage offers for ways that universities create access as an afterthought.[14] The essence of his critique is that retrofitting often brings with it additional barriers, inconveniences, or forms of exclusion. To use one of his examples, it is possible to provide some degree of access to a building by adding a ramp at the end of a winding path that is difficult to navigate. But this is far less satisfactory than the access offered by a straight ramp that is part of the building's initial design and construction. It may be useful to consider how tolerance for error might introduce analogous issues in the classroom. Let's say I assign my students a report or reflection, such as analyzing a film's depiction of disability. I integrate tolerance for error into the assignment both by offering the students various ways to complete it (text, video, audio) and by taking a broad perspective on what can count as a complete submission. From time to time, I will receive a submission that does not meet the basic expectations of the assignment at all. Rather than giving the student a failing grade, I will ask them to redo the assignment. I could see this application of tolerance for error introducing a range of barriers and inconveniences. The student has to put in additional time to complete a new assignment, even though they may not have been at fault in misreading the expectations. As the instructor, I have to do additional labor to assess two separate submissions for the same assignment.

One possibility is to accept that while tolerance for error is a form of retrofitting, it is sometimes necessary, and the best we can do is attempt to limit the logistic burdens it brings. So I might ask the student to revise only specific sections of the assignment. Another way to apply tolerance for error is to find ways of accepting the error in the wider context of the course. I characterize this as a more radical version of tolerance for error, in which the instructor accepts the consequences of the misunderstanding and revises their approach going forward. In this case, I might give the student feedback about how their assignment didn't meet expectations, confirm their achievement of the learning outcomes using a low-effort method like a conversation, and not require them to resubmit the assignment.

Access Friction

In the introduction to this book, we discussed an instance where there was a potential conflict between the access needs of two different neurodivergent students. For example, a student with ADHD might benefit from the use of a timer that counts down the remaining time for an activity and plays a sound once that time is over. However, a dyslexic student might need additional time to read and process material, and become anxious if a timer is used to alert students to the end of an activity. Autistic students could also become distressed by the sounds, especially if they are loud. Some other students might be neurotypical or have a combination of identities that means they have complex relationships to timers, loud sounds, and speeded activities in the classroom. What should we do when a certain decision in the classroom provides greater access for one student or group but creates barriers for others? This is the phenomenon called "access friction."

I was first introduced to the phrase by Arley McNeney—a teacher, scholar, disability advocate, and Paralympian who sadly passed away in 2023. McNeney posted on the social media site that was then called Twitter about a situation in her own classroom where one student needed a structured schedule for assignments, and another needed flexibility. There have been a few other definitions of the term "access friction" that differ from "conflicting access needs." Disabled scholar Liz Jackson uses the phrase as a way to describe the friction that occurs when we try to include disabled people in environments that were not built or intended for them.[15] It can also describe a situation in which nondisabled people attempt to provide access in a way that is not actually helpful to or desired by disabled people (what Jackson terms a "disability dongle"). Before we even consider *conflicting* needs, sometimes disabled people's *very presence* creates friction. I think many instructors have had the experience of a student coming to them with an access need that they had never anticipated, and at least momentarily feeling a loss of momentum as they reevaluate their teaching plans.

Following McNeney, I use the term "access friction" to describe a situation in which people have seemingly *opposing* access needs. Even though during this discussion we will consider access friction in an educational context, the phenomenon is far from restricted to learning environments (e.g., a person who has a service dog is seated next to someone with dog allergies in a restaurant or office). Highlighting one of the many potential caveats to the practice of UDL, I often encounter access friction when I invite students to choose from a variety of ways to demonstrate their knowledge or participate in a class activity. What happens when one student has difficulty accessing another student's contribution to the class? What about when only one room or type of technology is available for a class, and students have differing needs with respect to light and sound?

Because discussions about access frequently focus on disability, the term "access friction" is often linked to disability. But it could be used to describe any situation in which legitimate needs or preferences compete in a classroom, even if they are not related to disability. While active learning methods are an evidence-based strategy for student engagement, and thus beneficial to many students' learning, those who experience difficulty with spontaneous group interactions may find this to be a barrier with some active learning activities. This likely affects some neurodivergent students but could also involve international and multilingual students.[16]

How is access friction likely to manifest in neurodiverse classrooms and when we are teaching in the neurodiversity paradigm? How should we respond to access friction that arises in our classrooms? On the first of these questions, we might start by saying that access friction is virtually guaranteed in neurodiverse classrooms, given that such spaces will contain a mix of neurotypical and neurodivergent students with different neurotypes. Additionally, the instructor may be neurodivergent or have other access needs which could conflict with various student needs.

When I initially determined that access friction is an important consideration when we are teaching in the neurodiversity paradigm, I looked more closely at some texts by neurodivergent writers and teachers. I noticed that access friction is often discussed, if not always under that exact name. For example, Walker's essay on how to teach a class about autism starts by discussing how to consider access needs without automatic reliance on disability services, and then states that "conflicts between access needs should be negotiated in class as part of the learning process."[17] For Walker, the existence of access friction was obvious enough to simply note its existence and launch right into examples and solutions. He writes,

> For instance, I often get students who need to take notes on laptops, tablets, or other electronic devices, because they need the notes in order to retain information but they can't write quickly enough by hand. Personally, I can't focus on speaking and listening to the class while someone next to me is noisily tap-tap-tapping away at a keyboard. So, right at the beginning of the first day of class (when I'm teaching in person rather than online), I tell students that they're welcome to type during class as long as they don't sit too close to me—there's a "no typing zone" around the front of the room where I'm positioned, and a "typing zone" across the room from me. This works for everyone—and more importantly, it immediately provides students with

> an example of what access needs are and how they can be civilly negotiated.[18]

It is notable that Walker mentions both the idea of access friction—some students need to type in order to take notes, and the additional noise of the typing makes it difficult for her to concentrate on her own tasks—and the fact that he as the instructor has his own access needs. The first time I read this passage several years ago, I realized how challenging some of the background noises in the classroom are for me as an instructor. Walker and I are both Autistic, and many Autistic people have sensory processing differences and sensitivities.

Walker's example demonstrates that the concept of access friction is conceptually linked to the neurodiversity paradigm, or perhaps more broadly to the social model of disability. As we have discussed, the neurodiversity paradigm, which Walker himself first introduced, can be summarized as the idea that there is not fundamentally one right or best type of thinking, behavior, or communication. Usually, applying the neurodiversity paradigm can shift our perspective on how neurodivergence is often pathologized, and it helps us see that neither neurodivergence nor neurotypicality is inherently superior. And if no particular cognitive style is inherently superior, the paradigm can also help us see that no particular needs or preferences that result from a given cognitive style are inherently superior either.

Access friction, I would argue, is primarily a useful description of the conflicts that may occur in the classroom or elsewhere if we start from the assumptions that there are multiple access needs, they sometimes conflict, *and* there is not necessarily a hierarchy of these needs. If it were obvious which access needs were more important, there would be less friction, or potentially none at all. For example, if Walker determined that his own need to limit typing noise was the most important in the classroom, there would be less to negotiate, but the students affected would have to accept less access to the tools they need for learning. Access friction arises in situations where we do recognize differing needs as valid and have to decide how to ensure access for different people.

A FEW EXAMPLES OF ACCESS FRICTION

As mentioned earlier, my introduction to the concept of access friction was a Twitter thread by McNeney in which she gave a "student who needs weekly deadlines for structure" and "a student who needs flexibility" as a potential source of access friction.[19] Because many neurodivergent students have differences in executive functioning and attention, it is reasonable to expect different needs related to due dates and structure. Highly structured course designs with frequent due dates are often reported as being beneficial for students with ADHD.[20] Differently neurodivergent students may need more flexibility, with extra time to complete assignments.

While difficulty following established structures might seem like a minor inconvenience, I can personally attest to the intense frustration associated with trying to follow a structure that doesn't work for one's own thinking style. You may recall my story from the preface about how I tried and failed to prepare for a major exam in grad school as part of a study group and was only able to succeed on the second try by doing repeated retrieval practice on my own. Price recounts the story of Jeff, a student she tutored who tried earnestly to follow her advice for writing in stages, revising drafts, and ultimately producing a finished essay.[21] However, this process didn't work for him. He preferred one that involved a lot of thinking about his subject, and then finally writing out a complete essay beginning with the title and ending with the works cited. One of the simplest solutions to differing structural needs is to provide a looser framework such as scaffolding and not require strict adherence to a structure—a type of tolerance for error in handling access friction.

Friction also commonly occurs with respect to sensory needs. Some students benefit from sound amplification, backlit screens, and other intense representations of information, which can help them focus on relevant content and overcome distractions. Other students may be extremely sensitive to sound and light, and find them borderline painful when they are too intense. Discovering a middle ground where the sensory situation is at least tolerable for all students and then allowing students to duplicate content on their own devices could be a useful approach. As with most access friction, willingness to communicate needs is helpful. I was once participating in a small group activity in a very loud and busy room. I asked my group if we could conduct future group meetings in a small windowless room to reduce background noise. The group members agreed, but two weeks later one of the people in the group exasperatedly shared that he couldn't meet there anymore—it triggered his claustrophobia. I was upset that he had had to suffer for those few weeks, and we eventually found a larger and brighter, but still quiet meeting space.

Overall, one potentially beneficial mindset is to think about access friction as situations in which there are different, sometimes conflicting access needs, and acknowledge that we don't have to make these needs compete with each other.[22] Rather, members of a community can work together to attempt to satisfy various needs. Friction is part of the inclusion process, not an impediment to it. Aimi Hamraie and Kelly Fritsch write about the idea of "access as friction," a phrase that acknowledges that nearly all forms of access involve some struggle, and that pays tribute to the way disability activists have had to deliberately create friction (i.e., public protest and civil disobedience) to win access in the public sphere.[23] Another way of saying this is that leaning into friction—rather than avoiding it—can lead to growth and change for the better.[24] This may seem like an obvious point, but I find that it is actually quite challenging in much of the current academic environment, where we are often expected to view students as customers, and instructors as superhuman. In reality, a common source of access friction in the classroom is a difference between the access needs of students and those of the instructor. In all likelihood, navigating access friction will require open communication and flexibility from all members of the class community.

Our discussion of access friction here highlights a further example of the caveats to UDL and how we may build on its basic framework to more fully respond to neurodiversity. UDL as it is most commonly implemented takes the need to be able to perceive and easily process information most seriously in discussions of materials that the instructor provides to students, but rarely does it consider the accessibility of materials produced by students for each other or for instructors. I personally favor a version of UDL that creates significant flexibility for students in how they perceive information and participate in activities, *but one that also* asks them to invest in overall accessibility for the class community, not just themselves. Here is an example: In my introductory disability studies course, students have a choice of format for the final paper (essay, video, artistic work, PowerPoint, podcast, etc.) and are asked to share their final product with their colleagues. I ask the students to make sure that their final product is as accessible as possible to the rest of the class. If someone records a podcast, I ask them to at least provide a computer-generated transcript. If they produce a visual work of art, I ask them to provide a text summary of its appearance and their intentions in creating it. With this structure, I hope to move toward "collective access"[25] rather than just individual choice.

Overall, the approach I suggest for navigating access friction is to prioritize access while accepting that some friction is likely to remain. Recall Walker's example of access friction in his own classes: Some students need to type on computer keyboards in order to take notes, while he himself can't tolerate the additional noise of the tapping while trying to facilitate a class, leading him to designate a no-typing zone around him while encouraging typing in other areas of the room. This solution recognizes multiple legitimate needs, and reportedly "work[ed] for everyone" in the class.[26] However, it is notably not free of friction. The designation of typing and no-typing zones restricts where students can sit, and provides a daily reminder that parts of the classroom layout are based around access needs. A student who needs both to type and to be relatively close to the speaker to lip-read might only have a couple of suitable seats in the room, and they might need to discuss reserving one of those seats with the instructor and other students. What begins to emerge with this sustained consideration of access needs and access friction is a throughline of reflection and negotiation.

Takeaways

Teaching in the neurodiversity paradigm starts from the premise that neurodiversity exists, is potentially valuable, and is likely to introduce friction into learning environments. Universal Design—whether the original principles of Universal Design, UDL, or other frameworks based on Universal Design—provides an invaluable starting point for responding to neurodiversity in the classroom. However, there are enough caveats that additional ideas—such as the neurodiversity paradigm, double empathy, and access friction—are needed to aid us in navigating neurodiversity in the classroom. So much of teaching and learning is relational, and as we will see in chapter 6, so many of the challenging pressure points in teaching and learning are associated with social and collaborative activities. Teaching in the neurodiversity paradigm is ultimately a practice of navigating and negotiating diverse needs among students and instructors and working toward access. We can both anticipate and plan for access friction in teaching and learning while also acknowledging that our neurodiverse classrooms are unlikely to ever be completely friction-free.

Teaching Invitations

- Take most recommendations for teaching neurodivergent students with a grain of salt. They may be useful, but they may not apply to all neurodivergent students, even those in the specific group being addressed.

- Consider published strategies for teaching neurodivergent students, but also consider the value and opportunities of the neurodiversity that exists in your own teaching context. When students think and communicate differently from each other or from you, be curious about the potential value of these differences.
- Recognize that communication is difficult just as often as it is smooth. Consider ways to avoid locating these difficulties in individual differences and placing the blame on any one person.
- Making all expectations explicit from the start might be a difficult target to hit—use tolerance for error as a companion practice to handle differences in communication and understanding.
- Expect, recognize, and address access friction (or conflicting access needs). There will likely not be a perfect fix for access friction, but there may be a mutually agreeable compromise.

6

PRESSURE POINTS AND PRESSURE RELEASES

This chapter is about the teaching situations which often pose the greatest challenges when considering neurodiversity: group projects and assignments, practical learning situations like labs or simulations, and class activities that are highly discussion-based. We will build on chapter 5 by applying *teaching in the neurodiversity paradigm* to these pressure points. I use the term **pressure points** because these activities tend to be where there are many assumed norms and the stakes feel high enough for instructors and students that reconsidering these norms seems difficult or even impossible. Accordingly, it is not uncommon for these types of activities to be used as the "weeding out" mechanism for various programs of study, because they are thought to most closely mimic the job functions in that field. For example, if a student struggles in a patient simulation activity, how can they work as a physical therapist? These are situations in which a number of needs must be balanced and events tend to unfold in such a way that there are many interactions between students and instructors happening quickly. These are the pressure points that many instructors and students have told me are particularly challenging for neurodivergent people. To help further explain these challenges, let's turn to a term we discussed earlier in the book: **kairotic space**.

Pressure Points and Kairotic Spaces

In the introduction of this book, I wrote about my own identification with Margaret Price's concept of kairotic spaces. She defines these as:

> the less formal, often unnoticed, areas of academe where knowledge is produced and power is exchanged. A classroom discussion is a kairotic space, as is an individual conference with one's professor. Academic conferences are rife with kairotic spaces, including the question-and-answer sessions after panels, impromptu "elevator meetings," and gatherings at restaurants and bars on the periphery of formal conference events. Other examples from students' experiences might include peer response workshops, study groups, interviews for on-campus jobs, or departmental parties or gatherings to which they are invited."[1]

These spaces are kairotic—a descriptor derived from the classical rhetoric concept of *kairos* (having the quality of occurring at the right time)—because their primary distinguishing feature is their time-dependence. Price further defines kairotic spaces as having five different elements,[2] which I paraphrase as:

1. fast-unfolding and time-dependent
2. highly social and collaborative
3. high stakes

The term "kairotic space" is useful for describing any academic situation in which "spontaneity is combined with high levels of professional/academic impact."[3] Price is a teacher and scholar of the humanities, and she does not make extensive reference to the STEM disciplines in her discussion of kairotic spaces. So I want to make sure to also name labs, simulations, and other practical elements of these courses as additional kairotic spaces. One element of time-dependence that is relevant in the kairotic spaces of STEM disciplines (e.g., labs) is that they often involve specialized physical spaces or equipment that are not available for unlimited amounts of time or require staff supervision during their use. Thus, even when lab activities are not designed by the instructor to be time-limited, they often are functionally because of these logistic constraints.

Price suggests that kairotic spaces are challenging for students with mental disabilities to navigate, but I would like to provide a more detailed explanation of why this is the case. As noted, kairotic spaces are characterized by being time-dependent, highly social, and high stakes. The combination of these elements may create a perfect storm of barriers for a variety of neurodivergent students. Time-dependence can cause challenges for neurodivergent students—including those with ADHD, autism, learning disabilities, and anxiety—because there is a particular expectation about how quickly students will be able to complete tasks. Several disabilities associated with neurodivergence involve slower processing of certain information types compared to that of a person without the disability. Students with some disabilities may need more time to do tasks that involve reading, writing, or analyzing, and the stress and pressure of the time constraints may make it difficult for other students to complete the required tasks at all. Highly social or collaborative activities could present a challenge for neurodivergent students because they may have a different social style than neurotypical peers, they may have anxiety about working with peers or have experiences of being rejected by them, or they may feel like they are a burden to their peers because of their disability. The high stakes of kairotic activities could negatively affect neurodivergent students whose work or communication styles are viewed unfavorably by their peers.

Price also suggests that kairotic spaces and the challenges they present are understudied, and she hypothesizes that this is because their significance is underestimated by those who "move through them with relative ease."[4] In the preface to this book, I offered my own story of how kairotic spaces in my graduate programs caused me confusion and presented barriers. I hope the discussion in this chapter can further define kairotic spaces and help us understand them from the perspective of neurodiversity. This is a personal issue for me, as I have not always navigated kairotic spaces with ease.

One concept that could be helpful in thinking through how pressure could be released in some kairotic spaces is that of "real social skills," introduced by Ruti Regan. She is an Autistic rabbi and educator who has engaged in significant online writing and advocacy on disability, religion, politics, and parenting. If you have read this far in the book, you can tell that I am fond of humor, writing, and research that highlight the unhelpfulness of stereotypes about neurodivergent people. One of the most interesting and also most subtle examples of this genre that I have come across is Regan's blog *Real Social Skills*. It is difficult to determine the exact purpose of the blog (updated regularly from 2012 to 2022, during which time I followed it off and on), but its loose theme was taking a non-infantilizing, non-disparaging approach to providing information on social skills. In the first post on the blog, Regan notes that helping neurodivergent people develop and practice social skills is a common activity of therapists and other professionals who work with people with disabilities, but this is often done in an insensitive way that does not recognize personhood and agency. She writes, "It's important to remember that everyone is real. People who teach social skills to people with disabilities, or who provide therapy to autistic or intellectually disabled people, almost invariably are deficient in this vital social skill."[5] She reminds us that social skills are indeed very important, but that we often define the concept too narrowly.

Regan's blog is notable in that it takes what I might call an Autistic perspective on the idea of social skills. In every post, she challenges the idea that people will magically intuit what to do in various social situations, and she provides concise summaries of information people can use to understand the norms and procedures of social interactions (within a broad North American cultural context). Some of my favorites entries include "Interacting with a Person Walking a Dog" (it is generally acceptable to compliment a dog owner on the dog's cuteness and ask the dog's name or breed, and one may ask if it is OK to pet the dog, unless it is a working service dog)[6] and a post on useful phrases to say if you didn't hear what someone said.[7]

Some posts even deal with higher education. Regan offers an in-depth post about college syllabi, offering details about what sort of information one should be getting when "reading the syllabus." Regan informs readers that instructors may get "annoyed" if you email them to ask a question that they believe can be answered by reading the syllabus, such as when assignments are due or where to locate various readings. While I personally would counsel instructors against getting annoyed about this, it is undeniable that this does happen, and it is something that it might be useful to know. My favorite thing about this post is the way that Regan meticulously dissects various comments on syllabi statements and features and explains the common discrepancies between what they literally say and what they may actually mean. She writes,

> Sometimes there's more ambiguity that instructors realize, e.g.:
>
> - "Read Smith pp 1–15" might be ambiguous about *which* reading that is if there are multiple files listed as "Smith."
> - "Read the first chapter" could be unclear about whether it's the introduction or Chapter 1.

Furthermore, Regan provides detailed information about possible discrepancies between written and functional course policies.

> Sometimes the stated policies on the syllabus don't match an instructor's actual approach to teaching:

- Eg: Instructors are often required to include standard language reflecting school wide policies.
    - Some instructors copy and paste the required language without paying attention to it or having any actual intention of following it.
    - Eg: instructors may be required to paste in language that says something like "students with disabilities should contact the disability center for accommodations. No accommodations can be considered until documentation is provided."
    - In practice, many instructors who are required to say that on the syllabus are actually entirely willing to arrange for informal modifications if you talk to them directly. (eg: an instructor who usually gives written exams may have no objection to you using a computer instead.)[8]

Later in the post, Regan walks readers step by step through a process for clarifying some of these ambiguities. First, she writes, you should make sure to read the entire syllabus, remembering that the information you need may be in an unexpected place. Next, if you still can't find the answer to your question, you should contact an instructor, making sure to identify the right person to ask (instructor of record, teaching assistant, discussion leader). When you make contact, it might be useful to inform them about what information you could find in the syllabus, and why it didn't help to clarify this matter for you. While this process might not work for every single person, there is almost nowhere in higher education that one can get similar information or advice. Regan understands that saying, "Feel free to let me know if you have any questions" leaves a lot that students have to figure out themselves.

The real social skills perspective could be helpful in a higher education teaching context—especially around the pressure points that have the characteristics of kairotic spaces—because it offers a less value-laden perspective on norms. Regan is always careful to distinguish between norms or rules that pertain to safety or a larger goal (ask before petting a dog—you don't know if the dog likes to be petted) and those that are mere social convention (it's typically socially acceptable or appreciated to say that you think someone's dog is cute). Thinking back to my grad school experience, I would have appreciated advice phrased like this for the social elements of the program—something like "If social interactions are challenging, you can consider prioritizing interactions with your cohort and with potential mentors. Even if these feel hard, they can be useful in supporting you in certain ways down the line. If department happy hours feel challenging, that might be a situation where you make an effort to come for ten minutes and then leave."

Most importantly, the real social skills perspective assumes that someone who is having difficulty navigating a social situation has good intentions but needs more information on how to think about and move through a certain space. The remainder of this chapter considers several pressure points in the classroom and potential strategies for responding to neurodiversity in those contexts: group projects, labs and simulations, and class discussions. In addition to examining how each activity may qualify as a kairotic space, we will also consider what real social skills might be needed for the activity, as well as how concepts related to teaching in the neurodiversity paradigm could provide concrete teaching strategies.

Group Assignments or Projects

Group assignments are, as most instructors and faculty developers know, not only a pressure point in situations that involve neurodivergence but one of the more significant pressure points in teaching and learning as a whole. Collaborative learning is understood to be of value to students in many disciplines, especially in the STEM disciplines,[9] but there is also research that document students' negative attitudes toward collaborative learning.[10] Why are group assignments a pressure point in neurodiverse classrooms? When we consider group assignments as a part of Price's kairotic space concept, we can see how a combination of stakes and spontaneity create a potentially difficult environment for neurodivergent students.

Group assignments arguably meet all the requirements to be a kairotic space. Whether group meetings occur during class time or outside of class, group work is often expected to be done *during* group meetings—a spontaneous interaction. These interactions may be challenging for neurodivergent students to navigate because they could involve real-time processing of text (like documents or other media) or social interactions that present challenges. Time dependency adds another layer of complexity, since students collaborating on a group project must negotiate among themselves how to complete their project by the deadline. It is important that students' peers, and not only the instructor, acknowledge the needs of those who require the flexibility of additional time in learning situations—or even students who receive accommodations that allow them additional time. A student I was advising once told me that he printed out his accommodation letter to show his fellow group members in an engineering course, to help explain why he would sometimes need additional time on tasks. While some group activities have lower stakes, such as active learning activities used to punctuate a lecture, others have high stakes, like a final project or presentation worth a significant proportion of the course grade. If students are motivated by their final grade, power dynamics can easily emerge in which some students attempt to take control of the group's plan, or sideline students whose work or communication style seems like it will hold the group back. To illustrate how some of these different concerns could play out, here is a scenario that I use in many of my workshops on teaching and neurodiversity, which I call simply "the economics group project."

The Economics Group Project

Part 1: Chris teaches a lower-level economics course with a mix of majors and non-majors. During the first week of class, he announces that there will be a major group assignment that makes up 30 percent of the grade, and instructs students to form groups based on their seating arrangement at the desks that day. In an effort to help the students get to know each other more, he offers a short discussion prompt. Scanning the room, he sees that most students look engaged in the activity, so he works on setting up his laptop to display his lecture slides. Over the next several weeks, Chris provides group meeting time during class, circulating around the room to see if the groups have any questions. He isn't totally sure how to gauge some of the quieter groups' progress, so he sends out a survey on the course platform, asking students to provide an update on their group's project progress.

Chris receives the following reply from a student named Melinda:

> *Hi Professor,*
>
> *I am actually doing my project alone. When we formed groups during the first week of class I was part of a group but I wasn't included on the email thread to meet outside of class to work on the topic, and by the next week it seemed like they were going ahead without me. This is fine with me, since I am working by myself on a topic that I am passionate about: the pricing of textbooks for college students.*

Chris is surprised by this email—he thought he had clearly communicated that this was a group project. In his mind, he had not presented working independently as a valid option, but this student has gone ahead and done this anyway. After a few emails back and forth, Melinda tells Chris the names of the students she was originally grouped with before she was left off the email chain. Before class starts one day, Chris casually asks one of them, named Henri, about the initial formation of the group. Henri says that he remembers Melinda talking with the group on the first day, but that her email address was accidentally recorded wrong and she was left off the communications. Henri mentions that he and some of the other students feel that this is just as well because Melinda's "vibe seemed off" and they found her difficult to talk to. Henri is a little hard of hearing, and Melinda speaks very quietly, so he found it difficult to understand her when she talked. He assumed that Melinda had just found a different group to work with.

When I offer this case study to a group of instructors, I ask them at this point, "What might Chris do in this situation?" In the discussions, several themes tend to emerge. One is that Chris might want to reflect on the overall design and framing of this group project. Was there a reason why the groups needed to be formed based on the seating arrangement in the class, or could they have been put together in a different way, based on interests, schedules, or other factors? The project is a hefty 30 percent of the final grade, which could contribute to anxiety for students and a preference for a smoothly functioning group over an inclusive one. Participants also often point out that Chris has taken some admirable steps in supporting collaborative work (supplying a "get to know you" prompt, and checking in with individual groups about their progress). However, this clearly did not prevent the breakdown in communication that led to Melinda leaving the group. The reasons for Melinda's departure are not clear. Perhaps her fellow students did not enjoy working with her and either intentionally left her off the email chain or did so mistakenly and then neglected to correct the error. Perhaps there was a miscommunication that involved Henri's disability and Melinda's quiet voice. Perhaps Melinda really wanted to work on her own and took this as her opportunity to leave the group. At this point, Chris has a choice to either permit Melinda to work on her own, attempt to help her rejoin her initial group, or help her find a new one. As we will see in part 2, Chris chooses the last option.

Part 2: Chris asks to meet with Melinda during office hours. When they meet, he explains that the project is a group one and that working independently is not allowed. He doesn't mention the conversation with Henri, but he offers to help Melinda integrate into a different group of students who also happen to be doing a project on textbook pricing. He apologizes for not checking in earlier to make sure all the students had a group. Chris expects Melinda to accept this plan, but she discloses that she is Autistic and would like to work alone as an accommodation. According to Melinda, she struggles to connect with other students in these situations, and working in a group makes it harder for her to learn and complete her assignments.

The final scene here introduces what we might call a "pressure point within a pressure point": the possibility that a student will request accommodations that exempt them from having to participate in any collaborative activities at all. Based on my conversations with a number of disability services professionals, it seems that this accommodation is most frequently related to diagnoses of anxiety or autism. However, we may want to consider the possibility that a range of students may require these accommodations because the activities are often designed in an inaccessible way. Because of instructors' experience that students with certain diagnoses will require accommodations for group learning activities, they may continue to design these activities in a way that excludes or is otherwise difficult to navigate for neurodivergent students, resulting in a self-reinforcing cycle.

Furthermore, this is a perfect example of how a system of accommodations rather than accessible design does not necessarily provide an equitable outcome. In most cases, instructors include group activities in their courses because collaborative learning is understood to benefit students. Collaborative learning is an opportunity to make connections with peers, learn from others' perspectives, and have one's own views constructively challenged. If these activities are designed in a way that is not accessible to neurodivergent students and they receive an exemption as an accommodation, then they lose this opportunity. So, this is another example of how an appreciation of access friction and building in tolerance for error can positively contribute to inclusion for neurodivergent students in ways that are not always true for accommodations.

Let's say that Melinda, through disclosing her autism, receives an exemption from group projects either through the disability services office or because of flexibility that Chris provides of his own accord. If this were to occur after the initial events of the story related in part 1 above, we might say that Melinda's accommodation confirms her supposed communication and collaboration difficulties. However, several elements of the group project's design might have led the other students and Melinda to believe that it was more important to complete the project than to develop an effective collaboration between the group members. This misconception might have been avoided had Chris offered some frank, real social skills-style information at the beginning of the group project.

Group Work in the Neurodiversity Paradigm

To help students understand that collaboration is an important part of the assignment, Chris could say, "I'm asking you to do this group assignment because I believe you'll benefit from learning to work effectively in small groups. This might not be easy, but working together is the main goal. I'd much rather you reach out to me for support than dissolve your group!" Chris could further clarify how the group learning relates to the learning outcomes of the class, from his perspective. If the activity has no specific learning outcome that can only be fulfilled in a group, he might offer students the option to choose working alone as an alternative. If he decides that students must complete the assignment as part of a group, it is important to consider some of the challenges neurodivergent students may encounter. Autistic students and those with ADHD, a learning disability, or dyspraxia may have significant differences in executive functioning or the amount of time they need for various tasks. Recognizing these differences can help the instructor to design activities that are not hostile to these needs. For example, it may be really difficult for a group that contains neurodivergent students to achieve any sort of deliverable after a meeting of only one class period.

Designing group activities so that they include time for group members to get to know one another, establish communication, and initiate the project before any deliverables are due is an example of tolerance for error. The first few deliverables of the project can be lower stakes, so there is time to resolve any communication issues within a group before higher-stakes components are due. If Chris wanted to take the more radical perspective on tolerance for error mentioned in chapter 5, he could accept Melinda's decision to work on her own, and revise the assignment to clarify his group work policies in future semesters.

Access friction was a factor in this group's experience, if you look closely. Henri was hard of hearing, and aspects of Melinda's communication contributed to his difficulties in understanding her. Surfacing access needs early in the process of group work can help avoid interpreting access friction as ill intent. In this situation, if Henri was encouraged to share that he is hard of hearing, and was willing to do so, other students might be less likely to interpret an error such as leaving Melinda off the list as deliberate. Sensory needs should be taken seriously, and they can often be balanced if they are shared openly. Sharing more about needs in this situation could reveal common ground. In this situation, the group working in a small meeting room, rather than in the main classroom with significant background noise, would have probably benefited both Henri and Melinda. Based on the experience Chris had with this group, he might in the future anticipate the need for some groups to meet in smaller rooms and offer this choice up front.

Labs and Simulations

Labs and simulations are practical components of courses that either are connected to a particular more lecture-based or didactic course or stand on their own as requirements for a certain program. Labs are found primarily in the basic and applied sciences and engineering while simulations are often found in health-care fields, and both have elements of kairotic spaces. These courses often require students to complete a specific task within a defined amount of time, such as a chemistry experiment. Labs may be considered high stakes—at least in the sense that they make up a significant portion of the course grade—and they are often also highly time-dependent (the experiment or other activity needs to be conducted during the lab period). In addition, labs almost always involve group activities, whether in pairs or small groups of three of four students. While labs may be challenging for neurodivergent students to navigate because of their nature as kairotic spaces, they may also align well with neurodivergent students' strengths. For example, Autistic and ADHD students may possess the traits of attention to detail and hyperfocus that could well be useful in labs.

There is very interesting emerging literature on how students with disabilities experience various elements of STEM education, including the laboratory environment, and a fair number of such studies appear in the journal *CBE—Life Sciences Education*.[11] This journal should be commended for its commitment to publishing both work about the experiences of disabled students and work by researchers who themselves have disabilities. Some of this scholarship has recently begun to address labs as challenging learning environments for students with disabilities in general.[12] Lab equipment and furniture may not accommodate wheelchairs or mobility aids. Labs often require certain types of precise movements like pouring, leveling, measuring, reading small print, and manipulating fine instruments, which may not be possible for students with various disabilities. If we add these considerations to the ones raised above for neurodivergent students, I think we can say that labs are learning situations in which a lot of work needs to be done to ensure that students are set up for success.

Unfortunately, labs can be some of the least supported learning situations that students encounter. Perhaps more than any of the other pressure points discussed in this chapter, labs are an environment where students are expected to be able to work in groups with little preparation or clarification of communication style because of the imperative to complete the task before the lab period is over. While practices differ between instructors and institutions on whether students receive individual or collective grades for lab work conducted in groups, students are at least dependent on their group to supply the data that they later analyze as part of their reports or other deliverables.

Most of the same principles of group and collaborative work apply to labs and simulations, so I recommend using ideas from the previous case study to navigate challenges in these environments. Some things that might be unique to lab and simulation environments are small spaces and specialized instruments—students with dyspraxia or Tourette's could encounter challenges with these—and the social norms of a simulation exercise which requires role-playing. In chapter 5, we encountered the case study involving Cole, a student who found it difficult to adopt the mindset needed to participate in a role-playing activity. Instructors whose students share this difficulty might first consider how to respond with curiosity about the student's perspective, and offer ways to participate that do not assume the exercise is naturally engaging or easy for them: "Would you like to try having a script to read from? If that works for you, we can build that into future simulations."

Class Discussions and Small Seminars

Class discussions are a pressure point in neurodiverse classrooms because they often have unspoken expectations. Instructors sometimes tell me that they first registered that a student was neurodivergent because of their unexpected behavior during class discussions, whether they spoke too loudly or for too long, or did not speak at all. Price writes,

> Although the notion of a classroom "discussion" implies that it is open to all perspectives, this setting is in fact

> controlled by rigid expectations: students taking part in a "discussion" are expected to demonstrate their knowledge of the topic at hand, raise relevant questions, and establish themselves as significant, but not overly dominant, voices in a crowd of at least fifteen—and usually many more—other persons. Further complicating the transaction is the fact that different teachers have different expectations for the "script" of a classroom discussion.[13]

Price's description underscores that class discussions have elements of kairotic spaces because they are almost by definition rapidly unfolding and subject to a number of rules that are not always revealed.

One such rule is that contributions to the discussion are made verbally. Neurodivergent students sometimes report that a particular challenge is knowing when to jump in and talk and when to stop, especially when it seems like other students know how to do this intuitively.[14] Perhaps the consequences of jumping in at the "wrong" time are not actually so severe, but I think Price also hints at the ways we can actually make participating in class more difficult if we shy away from naming our expectations outright.

One technique I personally use to help students navigate class discussions is a discussion protocol, which I view as the real social skills for a class discussion—a flexible script for what to do, with useful information. The protocol itself could be as simple as writing down a response to a prompt and then reading it out loud, but it could also be a multi-step structure for guiding the flow of conversation. I often include two rounds of discussion in my protocols—one round for clarifying questions and then another for analysis. Most importantly, you might offer explanations of social conventions, such as "While there are no hard requirements for how long you should speak during a group conversation, if you are looking for a length to aim for, you could aim for about thirty seconds," and "Most times I will call on you before you speak, but I might also make eye contact with you to let you know it is your turn. If you have something to say, you should look in my direction." You could create a discussion protocol for your own teaching situation that is as flexible or detailed as you want. However, like any pedagogical feature, protocols require intentionality and frequent evaluation and troubleshooting. The protocol should ideally be responsive to the dynamics of the particular group you are working with. Most of the protocols I use were developed in response to some specific concern or observation but had to be adapted due to new students and new needs.

What if you have already taken steps to design your class discussions in the neurodiversity paradigm (like having multiple ways to participate and discussion protocols) but encounter student resistance? The following case study describes such a scenario.

Elissa and the Small Seminar

Elissa teaches a group of ten people in a women's and gender studies seminar. When she first started teaching this class, she used a modified Socratic method, modeling the course after one of her graduate school courses that she really enjoyed. After seeing how some students talked a lot in class and others spoke only very rarely, Elissa reached out to a teaching consultant for support with the design of the sessions. She also attended a workshop on equitable participation opportunities for disabled and neurodivergent students. Elissa now works with the assumption that offering multiple ways to participate in class (including speaking, non-speaking, and asynchronous options) and providing additional structure to the discussions can help support neurodivergent students. She does require that students participate in at least one way per class session.

This semester, Elissa outlines the format of the class discussions as part of the first session, explaining that for each discussion question, there will be free writing time followed by a structured discussion where students can either contribute verbally or using a document in Google Docs. One of the students, Jane, raises their hand and asks if the class can just use a "regular" discussion structure (i.e., more similar to their other seminars where students discuss the topics more organically). Jane says that they understand why Elissa's method might be helpful for neurodivergent students, but it feels overly prescriptive to them. Another student, Harriet, feels overwhelmed by the various options available. She asks if it would be possible to do an anonymous survey of the students to see what they all prefer in terms of discussion style.

Jane and Harriet seem to have some concerns that their own expression will be constrained by the discussion methods that Elissa is using. While they are willing to consider the need for inclusive approaches to discussion, they are wondering how the methods Elissa has chosen overlap with student needs within the class, including their own. There may be an element of access friction in their concerns—even though frameworks such as UDL suggest that multiple options for participation and interaction with materials offer greater accessibility, the increased cognitive load of these options may present challenges for some students.[15] We might take this as an opportunity to share the ideas of teaching in the neurodiversity paradigm with our students. Elissa might try to learn more about Harriet's and Jane's concerns or needs, and validate these. She could recognize that a different format from other courses may take some time to get used to. And she could highlight the reasons for this format, saying something like "I'm glad to hear you are open to helping create an inclusive environment for neurodivergent students. One thing I was thinking about when I planned the course is that not all neurodivergent students may have a diagnosis or choose to disclose. I think we can all benefit from some different options being available, especially as we are just getting to know each other at the beginning of the course."

Elissa also might remind the group that having options available doesn't require any student to use any particular one. Harriet and Jane are free to use whatever communication or expression methods work best for them—there is no one right way. She could add that her aim is to create a learning community that provides students with autonomy, and emphasizes respect for different choices or learning preferences. She could also establish a check-in point partway through the term when students can feed back on how the format of the class is working. Perhaps that would be a good time for the anonymous survey that Harriet suggested, as students will then have had more experience of one another, the instructor, and the various options for class participation.

This case study shows how our use of the neurodiversity paradigm in teaching does not necessarily depend on knowing that neurodivergent students or instructors are present. The interaction between Elissa, Jane, and Harriet offers an opportunity to highlight the value of multiple ways of thinking and communicating, as well as to consider some less obvious sources of access friction. If Elissa does conduct an anonymous survey and finds that, after trying her initial discussion format, all the students prefer a more spontaneous and verbal one, she might decide to make a change. Just as I mentioned that I adapt my discussion protocols in response to new students or conditions, Elissa might learn through the survey that the multiplicity of options has introduced an additional and unhelpful cognitive load for this group, and she can respond to that information.

Takeaways

There are undoubtedly more pressure points that share the elements of kairotic spaces beyond the ones discussed in this chapter. I hope that the three examples we discussed can provide useful principles for navigating pressure points that may be specific to your own teaching contexts. Applying these ideas to further learning situations—such as studio courses, and those that involve debates, mock trial proceedings, or even culinary demonstrations—will likely yield new insights about what information can help us set students up for success, where tolerance for error is needed, and what types of access friction are likely to arise in specific situations.

Teaching Invitations

- Consider explicitly naming when learning activities are designed to have a social element, and how students should proceed if this presents a barrier to their learning.
- Use the idea of *kairotic spaces* to predict potential pressure points in your teaching or other educational pursuits: Time-dependence, high stakes, and social intensity may contribute to barriers or friction.
- When introducing group activities, share with students the benefits of collaborative learning you hope to offer, but recognize that establishing effective communication and collaboration could take time.
- Encourage students to share communication and sensory needs—these could relate to modes of communication within the group, the location of group meetings, volume of sounds, or the need to move around a space.
- Consider using a discussion protocol to provide additional structure for class discussions.
- Engage students in conversation about the inclusive methods that you are trying out. Make sure that alternative options for participation—especially those designed to be inclusive of neurodivergent students—are framed as options rather than norms. And consider whether offering a variety of options might introduce additional access friction, such as increased cognitive load.

CONCLUSION

We've arrived at the end of our introduction to neurodiversity, which I hope is only the beginning of your journey in this area. There are several things that I hope you take away from this book, but I expect that you will also have reactions and new questions that emerge from the interaction of this book's content with your own experiences and interests. In this conclusion, we'll review the most important points of this book followed by three final invitations. These invitations relate to how this book's ideas affirm or challenge your teaching and learning practice, to your own goals for integrating what you have learned into your teaching, and to how you can apply some of this learning outside your work as an educator.

The History, Terminology, and Theories of Neurodiversity Help Us See Our Students, Colleagues, and Selves as Whole People

Throughout the book, we have defined and applied the terms "neurodiversity," "neurodivergent," "neurotypical," and others in ways that acknowledge their histories. I hope you'll take away a few things from this experience. Primarily, the term "neurodivergent" and its associated identity aim to provide an alternative to specific medical diagnoses. However, not all people who could plausibly apply the term to themselves will want to do so. Some of the ideas of the neurodiversity movement and work by neurodivergent researchers can inform our practice as educators in useful ways whether or not we ourselves or our students identify as neurodivergent or as having a disability. For example, what would it look like to approach miscommunications or misunderstandings first as differences that need to be negotiated, rather than one-sided deficits?

"Neurodivergence" is Much More an Umbrella Term or Coalition than One Clearly Defined Experience

One of my goals in writing this book was to make sure readers recognize that "neurodivergence" is a general term for cognition that differs from societal norms and does not refer to any specific condition or diagnosis. Not only is it important to keep this idea in mind as more of our students may identify as neurodivergent, but it also helps us see how teaching neurodivergent students or working with neurodivergent colleagues will necessarily involve navigating multiple needs and negotiating between different ways of thinking, behaving, and communicating. Our neurodiversity-affirming practice can include both learning about individual neurotypes and building skills for responding to wider neurodiversity in the classroom: recognizing the value in different ways of thinking, taking a humble and less deficit-based approach to communication challenges, and remembering that neurodiversity often brings friction.

We Can Expect and Address Friction While Teaching in the Neurodiversity Paradigm, Though We Can Never Remove It Entirely

When we respond to access friction, we can aim to maximize access for different people in the learning community through a process of negotiation. Such friction is not likely to go away entirely, but it might take on a more benign form, like people occupying different areas of a classroom or compromising about the sound level in a session. Access friction shows us that inclusion is a journey rather than a destination because of the variability of access needs, their dynamic nature, and the reality of logistic and space constraints. So many instructors I work with have told me that learning the term "access friction" allowed them to name a phenomenon they had experienced countless times but never had a word for. I hope our discussion of access friction has provided you with a new or updated way to think about access conflicts and potential responses to them.

The Neurodiversity Movement Relied On and Prioritized the Leadership of Neurodivergent People

Without the efforts of self-advocates, we wouldn't have the valuable ideas about neurodiversity that we have explored in this book. This importance of neurodivergent leadership is easily transferable to higher education contexts. As more and more students identify themselves as neurodivergent, often as a positive identity, we have the opportunity to invite neurodivergent students, staff, and faculty to play a central role in campus policies and initiatives for neurodivergent people. Consistent with this book's focus on there being no one right way, I think it is important to note that effective leadership does not necessarily take any one form, and it may not closely align with typical academic leadership roles like serving on committees or taking on administrative responsibilities. Leadership among neurodivergent people could look more like connecting neurodivergent students to neurodivergent faculty and staff members, and establishing a neurodivergent affinity group for students or staff and faculty.

My final three invitations for you are intended to take your thinking about neurodiversity from the narrower context of your educational work to your life more generally. There is of course no right way to answer these questions; some options might be pondering them or writing about them on finishing this book then returning to them some time later, or discussing them with friends or colleagues.

- How do the ideas and suggestions in the book affirm your current approach to teaching? How do they challenge it?
- What have you learned in this book that has motivated you to change something, either in your work or life more generally? What have you learned that has motivated you to keep doing something you are already doing?
- What does neurodiversity mean to you? How can using the concept contribute to your personal development, relationships with family and friends, and navigation of kairotic spaces?

A Final Word: "Introduction"

This book is titled *Classroom Mindscapes: An Introduction to Neurodiversity for Educators*, and it is intended to be just that: an introduction. While I hope that it has provided both the information and opportunities for reflection to help you either start or continue your learning journey with neurodiversity, there are a number of future directions that your learning could take. The book gives a particular perspective—mine—on neurodiversity and its importance for educators. This is far from the only important perspective. As you continue learning about neurodiversity, I encourage you to engage with other perspectives, including those that may challenge the ideas laid out in this book. A great place to start is conversations with neurodivergent students and colleagues, as well as the published perspectives of neurodivergent people and their allies.

In the speech that became the essay Don't Mourn for Us, Jim Sinclair tells their audience that non-Autistic parents raising an Autistic child might experience quite a lot of challenges and friction.[1] The differences between parent and child could be as stark as an alien and an earthling, but the relationship is still essential. Sinclair continues, “if that prospect excites you, then come join us, in strength and determination, in hope and in joy. The adventure of a lifetime is ahead of you.” I thank you for embarking on this adventure with me.

NOTES

Introduction

1. Price, *Mad at School: Rhetorics of Mental Disability and Academic Life*, 60.

2. Price uses the term "mental disabilities" throughout the book. For her, the term covers both characteristics I might term "neurodivergent" and the broader category of cognitive and psychiatric disabilities.

3. Smagorinsky, "Neurodiversity and the Deep Structure of Schools," 4.

4. Hubrig, "More than Accessibility: A Call for Disability Literacy."

5. Price, *Mad at School*; Price, *Crip Spacetime: Access, Failure, and Accountability in Academic Life.*

6. Walker, *Neuroqueer Heresies: Notes on the Neurodiversity Paradigm, Autistic Empowerment, and Postnormal Possibilities.*

7. Walker, *Neuroqueer Heresies*, 19.

8. Irish, "How to Make Room for Neurodivergent Professors"; Pryal, "Should You Seek an Adult Diagnosis of Neurodivergence?"; Schaefer and Sanchez, "Shining a Light on Neurodiversity in Higher Ed"; Pope-Ruark et al., *Of Many Minds: Neurodiversity and Mental Health Among University Faculty and Staff.*

9. Rodriguez and Silverman, "Horizontal Mentoring," 249.

10. Dolmage, *Academic Ableism: Disability and Higher Education.*

11. Dolmage, *Academic Ableism*, 145.

12. Kapp, ed., *Autistic Community and the Neurodiversity Movement: Stories from the Frontline.*

13. Sinclair, Don't Mourn for Us.

14. Kuder et al., *College Success for Students on the Autism Spectrum: A Neurodiversity Perspective.*

15. Costa, *An Educator's Guide to ADHD: Designing and Teaching for Student Success.*

16. Oslund, *Supporting College and University Students with Invisible Disabilities: A Guide for Faculty and Staff Working with Students with Autism, AD/HD, Language Processing Disorders, Anxiety, and Mental Illness.*

17. Walker, *Neuroqueer Heresies*, 17.

18. Kapp, "Introduction," 1–19.

Chapter 1

1. Andrews et al., "The Evolution of Disability Language: Choosing Terms to Describe Disability," 101328.

2. Hubrig, "More than Accessibility: A Call for Disability Literacy."

3. Dolmage, *Academic Ableism: Disability and Higher Education*; Dolmage, "Disabled upon Arrival: The Rhetorical Construction of Disability and Race at Ellis Island."

4. Giroux, "Introduction: Literacy and the Pedagogy of Political Empowerment," 6.

5. Walker, *Neuroqueer Heresies.*

6. Kapp, "Introduction," 1–19.

7. Singer, "Why Can't You Be Normal for Once in Your Life?: From a 'Problem with No Name' to a New Category of Disability."

8. Singer, "Why Can't You Be Normal for Once in Your Life?," 64.

9. Singer, "Why Can't You Be Normal for Once in Your Life?," 64.

10. Botha et al., "The Neurodiversity Concept Was Developed Collectively: An Overdue Correction on the Origins of Neurodiversity Theory."

11. Dekker, "A Correction on the Origin of the Term 'Neurodiversity.'"

12. Tisoncik, "Autistics.Org and Finding Our Voices as an Activist Movement," 65–76.

13. "Institute for the Study of the Neurologically Typical."

14. Silberman, *Neurotribes*, 440.

15. Kapp, "Introduction," 1–19.

16. Silberman, *Neurotribes*, 343.

17. Wells, "I Am Autistic."

18. Walker, *Neuroqueer Heresies*; Asasumasu, "PSA from the Actual Coiner of 'Neurodivergent.'"

19. Aylward et al., "Racial, Ethnic, and Sociodemographic Disparities in Diagnosis of Children with Autism Spectrum Disorder"; Driver and Chester, "The Presentation, Recognition and Diagnosis of Autism in Women and Girls."

20. Kapp, "How Social Deficit Models Exacerbate the Medical Model: Autism as Case in Point."

21. Taboas et al., "Preferences for Identity-First versus Person-First Language in a US Sample of Autism Stakeholders."

22. Kapp, "How Social Deficit Models Exacerbate the Medical Model."

23. Cherewick and Matergia, "Neurodiversity in Practice: A Conceptual Model of Autistic Strengths and Potential Mechanisms of Change to Support Positive Mental Health and Wellbeing in Autistic Children and Adolescents."

24. Hallowell and Ratey, *ADHD 2.0: New Science and Essential Strategies for Thriving with Distraction—from Childhood through Adulthood.*

25. Garnier-Dykstra et al., "Self-Reported Adult Attention-Deficit/Hyperactivity Disorder Symptoms among College Students."

26. Hotez et al., "A National Cross-Sectional Study of the Characteristics, Strengths, and Challenges of College Students with Attention Deficit Hyperactivity Disorder."

27. Levinovitz, "Do Colleges Provide Too Many Disability Accommodations?"

28. Costa, *An Educator's Guide to ADHD: Designing and Teaching for Student Success.*

29. Hotez et al., "A National Cross-Sectional Study of the Characteristics, Strengths, and Challenges of College Students with Attention Deficit Hyperactivity Disorder."

30. Costa, *An Educator's Guide to ADHD.*

31. Oslund, *Supporting College and University Students with Invisible Disabilities.*

32. Aherne, *The Pocket Guide to Neurodiversity.*

33. Tinker et al., "Estimating the Number of People with Tourette Syndrome and Persistent Tic Disorder in the United States."

34. eLife, "Neurodiversity in Academia: Time to Rethink Tourette's Syndrome."

35. Friedman et al., "A Qualitative Exploration of the Experiences of Self-Diagnosed Autistic Women and Gender-Diverse Individuals Who Are Not Pursuing an Autism Diagnosis."

36. Caron, "Don't Believe Everything You See About A.D.H.D. on TikTok."

37. Wise, *We're All Neurodiverse: How to Build a Neurodiversity-Affirming Future and Challenge Neuronormativity.*

38. Kapp, "Introduction."

39. Gillespie-Lynch et al., "Can We Broaden the Neurodiversity Movement without Weakening It? Participatory Approaches as a Framework for Cross-Disability Alliance Building."

40. Walker, *Neuroqueer Heresies*, 18.

41. Walker, *Neuroqueer Heresies.*

42. Reeves, "Toward a Neuroinclusive Campus."

43. Blyzniuk, "Neuroinclusion at UMA in Partnership with Landmark College."

44. Ferrigon and Tucker, "Person-First Language vs. Identity-First Language: An Examination of the Gains and Drawbacks of Disability Language in Society."

45. Ladau, "Why Person-First Language Doesn't Always Put the Person First."

46. Pryal, *A Light in the Tower: A New Reckoning with Mental Health in Higher Education*, 26.

47. Ferrigon and Tucker, "Person-First Language vs. Identity-First Language."

48. Haddon, *The Curious Incident of the Dog in the Night-Time.*

Chapter 2

1. Baker, *The Politics of Neurodiversity: Why Public Policy Matters.*

2. Kapp, "Introduction."

3. Sinclair, Don't Mourn for Us.

4. Kapp, "Introduction."

5. Kapp, "Introduction."

6. McCreary, "Beyond Backward Design, or, by the End of This Article, You Should Be Able to Imagine Some Alternatives to Learning Objectives."

7. Dekker, "From Exclusion to Acceptance."

8. Botha et al., "The Neurodiversity Concept Was Developed Collectively."

9. Sinclair, "Autism Network International: The Development of a Community and its Culture."

10. Sinclair, Don't Mourn for Us.

11. Goldrick-Rab and Stommel, "Teaching the Students We Have, Not the Students We Wish We Had."

12. Felten and Lambert, *Relationship-Rich Education: How Human Connections Drive Success in College.*

13. Kras, "The 'Ransom Notes' Affair: When the Neurodiversity Movement Came of Age."

14. Pryal, "How to Teach Your (Many) Neurodivergent Students."

15. Sander, "Seeking a Deft Touch for Students with Autism-Spectrum Disorders."

16. Milton, "On the Ontological Status of Autism: The 'Double Empathy Problem.'"

17. Kapp, "How Social Deficit Models Exacerbate the Medical Model."

18. Hudenko et al., "Laughter Differs in Children with Autism: An Acoustic Analysis of Laughs Produced by Children with and without the Disorder."

19. Kapp, "Profound Concerns about 'Profound Autism': Dangers of Severity Scales and Functioning Labels for Support Needs."

20. Cowen, "Michelle Dawson on Autism and Atypicality."

21. Smith, "'I Am a Minimally Speaking Autistic Person Who Was Not Expected to Go to College.' Now He's Getting His PhD."

22. Luterman, "Jordyn Zimmerman Is Redefining Communication as a Nonspeaking Advocate for Disability Rights."

23. Walker, *Neuroqueer Heresies*, 48.

24. Marinus et al., "A Special Font for People with Dyslexia: Does It Work and, If So, Why?"

25. Wise, *We're All Neurodiverse.*

26. Ne'eman and Pellicano, "Neurodiversity as Politics," 149.

27. Baker, *The Politics of Neurodiversity*, 21.

Chapter 3

1. "About ASAN—Autistic Self Advocacy Network."

2. Baker, *The Politics of Neurodiversity.*

3. Walker, *Neuroqueer Heresies*; Shakespeare, "The Social Model of Disability."

4. Walker, *Neuroqueer Heresies*, 60–61.

5. Walker, *Neuroqueer Heresies*, 65.

6. Walker, *Neuroqueer Heresies*, 68.

7. Kapp, "Introduction."

8. Dwyer, "The Neurodiversity Approach (Es): What Are They and What Do They Mean for Researchers?"; Dwyer et al., "Community Views of Neurodiversity, Models of Disability and Autism Intervention: Mixed Methods Reveal Shared Goals and Key Tensions."

9. Dwyer, "The Neurodiversity Approach (Es)."

10. Lierman, *The Struggle You Can't See: Experiences of Neurodivergent and Invisibly Disabled Students in Higher Education*; Oslund, *Supporting College and University Students with Invisible Disabilities.*

11. Lierman, *The Struggle You Can't See*, 46.

12. Colson and Smothers, "FAPE, LRE, and Related Laws: Implications for Inclusion and Co-Teaching," 1–2.

13. Heumann, "Our Fight for Disability Rights – And Why We're Not Done Yet."

14. Walker, *Neuroqueer Heresies*, 150.

15. Olsen et al., "The Disability Tax and the Accessibility Tax: The Extra Intellectual, Emotional, and Technological Labor and Financial Expenditures Required of Disabled People in a World Gone Wrong . . . and Mostly Online"; Konrad, "Access Fatigue: The Rhetorical Work of Disability in Everyday Life."

16. Hora, "On (Trying to) Work with a Nonapparent Disability in the Academic Workplace: Toward a True Inclusivity for Disabled Workers in Higher Education."

17. Wendell, *The Rejected Body: Feminist Philosophical Reflections on Disability*, 37.

18. Wise, *We're All Neurodiverse.*

19. Williamson, *Accessible America: A History of Disability and Design.*

20. Centre for Excellence in Universal Design, "The 7 Principles."

21. Rao et al., "Universal Design for Learning in Its 3rd Decade: A Focus on Equity, Inclusion, and Design."

22. Burgstahler, "Equal Access: Universal Design of Instruction."

23. Dolmage, *Academic Ableism*, 120.

24. King-Sears, "Universal Design for Learning: Technology and Pedagogy."

25. Burgstahler, "Equal Access."

26. Hogan and Sathy, *Inclusive Teaching: Strategies for Promoting Equity in the College Classroom.*

27. Copeland et al., "Helping Students by Using Transparent Writing Assignments."

28. Gobbo and Shmulsky, "Faculty Experience with College Students with Autism Spectrum Disorders: A Qualitative Study of Challenges and Solutions."

29. Kuder et al., *College Success for Students on the Autism Spectrum.*

30. Gobbo and Shmulsky, "Faculty Experience with College Students with Autism Spectrum Disorders," 5.

31. Gobbo and Shmulsky, "Faculty Experience with College Students with Autism Spectrum Disorders," 17.

32. Katz, *Teaching to Diversity: The Three-Block Model of Universal Design for Learning,* 14.

Chapter 4

1. Selingo, *Who Gets In and Why: A Year inside College Admissions;* Poon and Bastedo, *Rethinking College Admissions: Research-Based Practice and Policy.*

2. Armstrong and Hamilton, *Paying for the Party: How College Maintains Inequality;* Goldrick-Rab, "Paying the Price: College Costs, Financial Aid, and the Betrayal of the American Dream"; Zaloom, *Indebted: How Families Make College Work at Any Cost.*

3. Eyler, *Failing Our Future: How Grades Harm Students, and What We Can Do About It.*

4. Kezar et al., *The Gig Academy: Mapping Labor in the Neoliberal University;* Nzinga, *Lean Semesters: How Higher Education Reproduces Inequity.*

5. Smagorinsky, "Neurodiversity and the Deep Structure of Schools."

6. Smagorinsky, "Neurodiversity and the Deep Structure of Schools," 15.

7. Snyder and Mitchell, "Afterword—Regulated Bodies: Disability Studies and the Controlling Professions," 175.

8. Dolmage, *Academic Ableism.*

9. Dolmage, *Academic Ableism,* 9.

10. Posselt, *Inside Graduate Admissions: Merit, Diversity, and Faculty Gatekeeping.*

11. Posselt, *Inside Graduate Admissions,* 9.

12. Vidali, "Texts of Our Institutional Lives: Performing the Rhetorical Freak Show: Disability, Student Writing, and College Admissions."

13. Wei et al., "Postsecondary Pathways and Persistence for STEM versus Non-STEM Majors: Among College Students with an Autism Spectrum Disorder."

14. Clark and Talbert, *Grading for Growth: A Guide to Alternative Grading Practices that Promote Authentic Learning and Student Engagement in Higher Education.*

15. Jain, "Why Crip Assessment? Critical Disability Studies Theories to Advance Assessment for Inclusion," 32.

16. Pitts Donahoe, "What Is Ungrading? What Is Collaborative Grading?"

17. Kohn and Blum, *Ungrading: Why Rating Students Undermines Learning (and What to Do Instead).*

18. Carillo, *The Hidden Inequities in Labor-Based Contract Grading.*

19. Carillo, *The Hidden Inequities in Labor-Based Contract Grading,* 18.

20. Carillo, *The Hidden Inequities in Labor-Based Contract Grading,* 5–6.

21. Carillo, *The Hidden Inequities in Labor-Based Contract Grading,* 60.

22. Kryger and Zimmerman, "Neurodivergence and Intersectionality in Labor-Based Grading Contracts," 8.

23. Pace, "My Personal Experiences of Dyspraxia: Management Strategies and Resources for All."

24. Dolmage, *Academic Ableism,* 67.

25. Fairleigh Dickinson University, "COMPASS Program."

26. Marist University, "Accommodations and Accessibility: Learning Support Program."

27. Nachman, "'The Beacon on Campus': How an Autism-Specific Community College Support Program Addresses Ableism and Autism Acceptance."

28. Nachman, "'The Beacon on Campus,'" 37.

29. Rose and Meyer, *Teaching Every Student in the Digital Age: Universal Design for Learning.*

30. CAST, "The UDL Guidelines."

31. CAST, "UDL and the Learning Brain."

32. One key distinction between UDL (and its foundational concept of learner variability) and the concept of neurodiversity is that UDL focuses on variability among learners specifically, while neurodiversity focuses more generally on variation in how people think, behave, and communicate.

33. Rose and Meyer, *Teaching Every Student in the Digital Age,* 11.

34. Rao, "Inclusive Instructional Design: Applying UDL to Online Learning," 84.

35. Clouder et al., "Neurodiversity in Higher Education: A Narrative Synthesis"; Dwyer et al., "Building Neurodiversity-Inclusive Postsecondary Campuses: Recommendations for Leaders in Higher Education"; Hamilton and Petty, "Compassionate Pedagogy for Neurodiversity in Higher Education: A Conceptual Analysis."

36. Dwyer et al., "Building Neurodiversity-Inclusive Postsecondary Campuses."

37. Rose and Meyer, *Teaching Every Student in the Digital Age*; Meyer et al., *Universal Design for Learning: Theory and Practice.*

38. Rao et al., "Universal Design for Learning in Its 3rd Decade."

39. CAST, "Consideration 5.4: Address Biases Related to Modes of Expression and Communication."

Chapter 5

1. Walker, *Neuroqueer Heresies*, 78.

2. McKeon et al., "Promoting Academic Engagement for College Students with Autism Spectrum Disorder," 359.

3. McKeon et al., "Promoting Academic Engagement for College Students with Autism Spectrum Disorder," 358.

4. McKeon et al., "Promoting Academic Engagement for College Students with Autism Spectrum Disorder," 358.

5. Walker, *Neuroqueer Heresies*, 74.

6. Dolmage, "Universal Design: Places to Start."

7. Dolmage, *Academic Ableism: Disability and Higher Education*, 73.

8. Dolmage, *Academic Ableism*, 74.

9. Price, *Mad at School*, 87.

10. Lierman, *The Struggle You Can't See*, 71.

11. Milton, "On the Ontological Status of Autism," 884.

12. Winkelmes et al., *Transparent Design in Higher Education Teaching and Leadership: A Guide to Implementing the Transparency Framework Institution-Wide to Improve Learning and Retention.*

13. Parish, *Thank You, Amelia Bedelia.*

14. Dolmage, *Academic Ableism*, 67.

15. Jackson, "Honoring the Friction of Disability."

16. Rios, "Positioned as a Burden: Analyzing the Participation of Multilingual Students of Color in Undergraduate Mathematics Courses that Use Groupwork."

17. Walker, *Neuroqueer Heresies*, 152.

18. Walker, *Neuroqueer Heresies*, 152.

19. McNeney, "I've been thinking about how access friction impacts my course design."

20. Costa, "Systems Aren't Scary."

21. Price, *Mad at School*, 66–67.

22. Calling Up Justice, "Access Friction Explained."

23. Hamraie and Fritsch, "Crip Technoscience Manifesto," 10.

24. Cavanagh, "In Defense of Friction."

25. Berne et al., "Ten Principles of Disability Justice," 228.

26. Walker, *Neuroqueer Heresies*, 152.

Chapter 6

1. Price, *Mad at School*, 60.

2. Price, *Mad at School*, 61.

3. Price, *Mad at School*, 61.

4. Price, *Mad at School*, 63.

5. Regan, "Social Skill: Theory of Mind."

6. Regan, "Social Skill: Interacting with a Person Walking a Dog."

7. Regan, "Some Useful Phrases."

8. Regan, "'Read the Syllabus': Getting the Information You Need without Annoying Your Instructors."

9. Kober, *Reaching Students: What Research Says about Effective Instruction in Undergraduate Science and Engineering*; Goldsmith et al., "Overcoming the Barriers to Teaching Teamwork to Undergraduates in STEM."

10. Tucker and Abbasi, "Bad Attitudes: Why Design Students Dislike Teamwork."

11. Gin et al., "COVID-19 and Undergraduates with Disabilities: Challenges Resulting from the Rapid Transition to Online Course Delivery for Students with Disabilities in Undergraduate STEM at Large-Enrollment Institutions"; Gin et al., "Students with Disabilities in Life Science Undergraduate Research Experiences: Challenges and Opportunities"; Goldsmith et al., "Overcoming the Barriers to Teaching Teamwork to Undergraduates in STEM."

12. Jeannis et al., "Full-Participation of Students with Physical Disabilities in Science and Engineering Laboratories."

13. Price, *Mad at School*, 59.

14. Salvatore et al., "'Not a Cookie Cutter Situation': How Neurodivergent Students Experience Group Work in Their STEM Courses."

15. Anastasiou et al., "A Critical Analysis of Theoretical Underpinnings of Universal Design for Learning."

Conclusion

1. Sinclair, Don't Mourn for Us.

REFERENCES

Aherne, Daniel. *The Pocket Guide to Neurodiversity.* Jessica Kingsley Publishers, 2023.

Anastasiou, Dimitris, Andrew L. Wiley, and James M. Kauffman. "A Critical Analysis of Theoretical Underpinnings of Universal Design for Learning." *Exceptionality* 33, no. 3 (2025): 145–62.

Andrews, Erin E., Robyn M. Powell, and Kara Ayers. "The Evolution of Disability Language: Choosing Terms to Describe Disability." *Disability and Health Journal* 15, no. 3 (2022): 101328.

Armstrong, Elizabeth A., and Laura T. Hamilton. *Paying for the Party: How College Maintains Inequality.* Harvard University Press, 2013.

Asasumasu, Kassiane. "PSA from the Actual Coiner of 'Neurodivergent.'" Tumblr. *Lost in My Mind TARDIS* (blog). Accessed February 26, 2025. https://sherlocksflataffect.tumblr.com/post/121295972384/psa-from-the-actual-coiner-of-neurodivergent.

Autistic Self Advocacy Network. "About ASAN—Autistic Self Advocacy Network," May 26, 2011. https://Autisticadvocacy.org/about-asan/.

Aylward, Brandon S., Diana E. Gal-Szabo, and Sharief Taraman. "Racial, Ethnic, and Sociodemographic Disparities in Diagnosis of Children with Autism Spectrum Disorder." *Journal of Developmental & Behavioral Pediatrics* 42, no. 8 (2021): 682–89.

Baker, Dana Lee. *The Politics of Neurodiversity: Why Public Policy Matters.* Lynne Rienner Publishers, 2011.

Berne, Patricia, Aurora Levins Morales, David Langstaff, and Sins Invalid. "Ten Principles of Disability Justice." *WSQ: Women's Studies Quarterly* 46, no. 1 (2018): 227–30.

Blyzniuk, Roman. "Neuroinclusion at UMA in Partnership with Landmark College." University of Maine at Augusta, May 21, 2024. https://video.maine.edu/media/Neuroinclusion+at+UMA+in+partnership+with+Landmark+College/1_unn004ci.

Botha, Monique, Robert Chapman, Morénike Giwa Onaiwu, Steven K. Kapp, Abs Stannard Ashley, and Nick Walker. "The Neurodiversity Concept Was Developed Collectively: An Overdue Correction on the Origins of Neurodiversity Theory." *Autism* 28, no. 6 (2024): 1591–94.

Burgstahler, Sheryl. "Equal Access: Universal Design of Instruction." DO-IT, University of Washington, April 7, 2008. https://doit.uw.edu/brief/equal-access-universal-design-of-instruction/

Calling Up Justice. "Access Friction Explained," May 7, 2023. https://callingupjustice.com/access-friction-explained/.

Carillo, Ellen C. *The Hidden Inequities in Labor-Based Contract Grading.* University Press of Colorado, 2021.

Caron, Christina. "Don't Believe Everything You See About A.D.H.D. on TikTok." *New York Times,* March 19, 2025. https://www.nytimes.com/2025/03/19/well/mind/adhd-videos-tiktok-misinfo.html.

CAST. "UDL and the Learning Brain," 2018. https://www.cast.org/resources/tips-articles/udl-learning-brain-neuroscience/.

———. "Consideration 5.4: Address Biases Related to Modes of Expression and Communication," 2024. https://udlguidelines.cast.org/action-expression/expression-communication/bias/.

———. "The UDL Guidelines," 2024. https://udlguidelines.cast.org/.

Cavanagh, Sarah Rose. "In Defense of Friction." *Once More, With Feeling* (blog), April 22, 2024. https://sarahrosecav.substack.com/p/in-defense-of-friction

Centre for Excellence in Universal Design, "The 7 Principles," n.d. https://universaldesign.ie/about-universal-design/the-7-principles.

Cherewick, Megan, and Michael Matergia. "Neurodiversity in Practice: A Conceptual Model of Autistic Strengths and Potential Mechanisms of Change to Support Positive Mental Health and Wellbeing in Autistic Children and Adolescents." *Advances in Neurodevelopmental Disorders* 8, no. 3 (2024): 408–22.

Clark, David, and Robert Talbert. *Grading for Growth: A Guide to Alternative Grading Practices that Promote Authentic Learning and Student Engagement in Higher Education.* Taylor & Francis, 2023.

Clouder, Lynn, Mehmet Karakus, Alessia Cinotti, María Virginia Ferreyra, Genoveva Amador Fierros, and Patricia Rojo. "Neurodiversity in Higher Education: A Narrative Synthesis." *Higher Education* 80, no. 4 (2020): 757–78.

Colson, Tori L., and Moriah J. Smothers. "FAPE, LRE, and Related Laws: Implications for Inclusion and Co-Teaching." *Kentucky Teacher Education Journal: The Journal of the Teacher Education Division of the Kentucky Council for Exceptional Children* 5, no. 1 (2018).

Copeland, David E., M. A. Winkelmes, and K. Gunawan. "Helping Students by Using Transparent Writing Assignments." In *Integrating Writing into the Psychology Course: Strategies for Promoting Student Success*, edited by Tara L. Kuther. Society for the Teaching of Psychology, 2018: 26–37.

Costa, Karen. *An Educator's Guide to ADHD: Designing and Teaching for Student Success.* Johns Hopkins University Press, 2026.

———. "Systems Aren't Scary," n.d. https://karenraycosta.medium.com/systems-arent-scary-e55d8ac63bc7.

Cowen, Tyler, host, *Conversations with Tyler,* podcast, episode 46, "Michelle Dawson on Autism and Atypicality," August 1, 2018. https://conversationswithtyler.com/episodes/michelle-dawson/.

Dekker, Martijn. "From Exclusion to Acceptance: Independent Living on the Autistic Spectrum." In *Autistic Community and the Neurodiversity Movement*, edited by Steven K. Kapp. Palgrave Macmillan, 2020: 41–49.

———. "A Correction on the Origin of the Term 'Neurodiversity.'" *Martijn "McDutchie" Dekker's Blog* (blog), July 13, 2023. https://www.inlv.org/2023/07/13/neurodiversity-origin.html.

Dolmage, Jay. "Disabled upon Arrival: The Rhetorical Construction of Disability and Race at Ellis Island." *Cultural Critique* 77 (2011): 24–69.

———. "Universal Design: Places to Start." *Disability Studies Quarterly* 35, no. 2 (2015).

———. *Academic Ableism: Disability and Higher Education.* University of Michigan Press, 2017.

Driver, Bethany, and Verity Chester. "The Presentation, Recognition and Diagnosis of Autism in Women and Girls." *Advances in Autism* 7, no. 3 (2021): 194–207.

Dwyer, Patrick. "The Neurodiversity Approach(es): What Are They and What Do They Mean for Researchers?" *Human Development* 66, no. 2 (2022): 73–92.

———, Ava N. Gurba, Steven K. Kapp, Elizabeth Kilgallon, Lynnette H. Hersh, David S. Chang, Susan M. Rivera, and Kristen Gillespie-Lynch. "Community Views of Neurodiversity, Models of Disability and Autism Intervention: Mixed Methods Reveal Shared Goals and Key Tensions." *Autism* 29, no. 9 (2024): 2297–314.

———, Erica Mineo, Kristin Mifsud, Chris Lindholm, Ava Gurba, and TC Waisman. "Building Neurodiversity-Inclusive Postsecondary Campuses: Recommendations for Leaders in Higher Education." *Autism in Adulthood* 5, no. 1 (2023): 1–14.

eLife. "Neurodiversity in Academia: Time to Rethink Tourette's Syndrome." eLife Sciences Publications Limited, May 7, 2024. https://elifesciences.org/interviews/fd51b6c1/laura-beljaars-and-diana-beljaars.

Eyler, Joshua. *Failing Our Future: How Grades Harm Students, and What We Can Do About It.* Johns Hopkins University Press, 2024.

Fairleigh Dickinson University. "COMPASS Program," n.d. https://www.fdu.edu/academics/colleges-schools/psychology/compass-program/.

Felten, Peter, and Leo M. Lambert. *Relationship-Rich Education: How Human Connections Drive Success in College.* Johns Hopkin University Press, 2020.

Ferrigon, Phillip, and Kevin Tucker. "Person-First Language vs. Identity-First Language: An Examination of the Gains and Drawbacks of Disability Language in Society." *Journal of Teaching Disability Studies* 1 (2019): 1–12.

Friedman, Alina, Aspasia Paltoglou, and Rossella Sorte. "A Qualitative Exploration of the Experiences of Self-Diagnosed Autistic Women and Gender-Diverse Individuals Who Are Not Pursuing an Autism Diagnosis." *Neurodiversity* 2 (2024): 27546330241307828.

Garnier-Dykstra, Laura M., Gillian M. Pinchevsky, Kimberly M. Caldeira, Kathryn B. Vincent, and Amelia M. Arria. "Self-Reported Adult Attention-Deficit/Hyperactivity Disorder Symptoms among College Students." *Journal of American College Health* 59, no. 2 (2010): 133–36.

Gillespie-Lynch, Kristen, Patrick Dwyer, Christopher Constantino, Steven K. Kapp, Emily Hotez, Ariana Riccio, Danielle DeNigris, Bella Kofner, and Eric Endlich. "Can We Broaden the Neurodiversity Movement without Weakening It? Participatory Approaches as a Framework for Cross-Disability Alliance Building." In *Disability Alliances and Allies: Opportunities and Challenges,* edited by Allison C. Carey, Joan M. Ostrove, and Tara Fannon. Emerald Publishing Limited, 2020: 189–223.

Gin, Logan E., Frank A. Guerrero, Sara E. Brownell, and Katelyn M. Cooper. "COVID-19 and Undergraduates with Disabilities: Challenges Resulting from the Rapid Transition to Online Course Delivery for Students with Disabilities in Undergraduate STEM at

Large-Enrollment Institutions." *CBE—Life Sciences Education* 20, no. 3 (2021): ar36.

———, Danielle Pais, Katelyn M. Cooper, and Sara E. Brownell. "Students with Disabilities in Life Science Undergraduate Research Experiences: Challenges and Opportunities." *CBE—Life Sciences Education* 21, no. 2 (2022): ar32.

Giroux, Henry A. Introduction to *Literacy: Reading the Word and the World*, by Paulo Freire and Donaldo Macedo. Routledge, 2005: 1–27.

Gobbo, Ken, and Solvegi Shmulsky. "Faculty Experience With College Students With Autism Spectrum Disorders: A Qualitative Study of Challenges and Solutions." *Focus on Autism and Other Developmental Disabilities* 29, no. 1 (2014): 13–22.

Goldrick-Rab, Sara. *Paying the Price: College Costs, Financial Aid, and the Betrayal of the American Dream*. University of Chicago Press, 2016.

———, and Jesse Stommel. "Teaching the Students We Have, Not the Students We Wish We Had." *Chronicle of Higher Education*, December 10, 2018. https://www.chronicle.com/article/teaching-the-students-we-have-not-the-students-we-wish-we-had/.

Goldsmith, Gregory R., Miranda L. Aiken, Hector M. Camarillo-Abad, Kamal Diki, Daniel L. Gardner, Mario Stipčić, and Javier F. Espeleta. "Overcoming the Barriers to Teaching Teamwork to Undergraduates in STEM." *CBE—Life Sciences Education* 23, no. 2 (2024): es2.

Haddon, Mark. *The Curious Incident of the Dog in the Night-Time*. Red Fox, 2014.

Hallowell, Edward M., and John J. Ratey. *ADHD 2.0: New Science and Essential Strategies for Thriving with Distraction—from Childhood through Adulthood*. Ballantine Books, 2022.

Hamilton, Lorna G., and Stephanie Petty. "Compassionate Pedagogy for Neurodiversity in Higher Education: A Conceptual Analysis." *Frontiers in Psychology* 14 (2023): 1093290.

Hamraie, Aimi, and Kelly Fritsch. "Crip Technoscience Manifesto." *Catalyst: Feminism, Theory, Technoscience* 5, no. 1 (2019): 1–33.

Heumann, Judy. "Our Fight for Disability Rights – And Why We're Not Done Yet," TED Talk, Washington, DC, October 2016, 17 min., https://www.ted.com/talks/judith_heumann_our_fight_for_disability_rights_and_why_we_re_not_done_yet.

Hogan, Kelly A., and Viji Sathy. *Inclusive Teaching: Strategies for Promoting Equity in the College Classroom*. West Virginia University Press, 2022.

Hora, Matthew T. "On (Trying to) Work with a Nonapparent Disability in the Academic Workplace: Toward a True Inclusivity for Disabled

Workers in Higher Education." *Change: The Magazine of Higher Learning* 56, no. 5 (2024): 4–12.

Hotez, Emily, Kashia A. Rosenau, Priyanka Fernandes, Kevin Eagan, Lindsay Shea, and Alice A. Kuo. "A National Cross-Sectional Study of the Characteristics, Strengths, and Challenges of College Students with Attention Deficit Hyperactivity Disorder." *Cureus* 14, no. 1 (2022): e21520.

Hubrig, Ada. "More than Accessibility: A Call for Disability Literacy." *Sandbox: Short Papers, Big Ideas on Literacy and Learning* 1, no. 1 (2023). https://communityliteraciescollaboratory.com/sandbox/vol-1-issue-1/more-than-accessibility-a-call-for-disability-literacy.

Hudenko, William J., Wendy Stone, and Jo-Anne Bachorowski. "Laughter Differs in Children with Autism: An Acoustic Analysis of Laughs Produced by Children with and without the Disorder." *Journal of Autism and Developmental Disorders* 39, no. 10 (2009): 1392–400.

Institute for the Study of the Neurologically Typical. "Institute for the Study of the Neurologically Typical (archived version)," n.d. https://erikengdahl.se/autism/isnt/.

Irish, Bradley J. "How to Make Room for Neurodivergent Professors." *Chronicle of Higher Education*, March 2, 2023. https://www.chronicle.com/article/how-to-make-room-for-neurodivergent-professors.

Jackson, Liz. "Honoring the Friction of Disability," AIGA Design Conference 2019, April 4–6, 2019, posted June 7, 2019 by AIGAdesign, YouTube. https://www.youtube.com/watch?v=cZhiu-jGbdE.

Jain, Neera R. "Why Crip Assessment? Critical Disability Studies Theories to Advance Assessment for Inclusion." In *Assessment for Inclusion in Higher Education*, edited by Rolla Ajjawi, Joanna Tai, David Boud, and Trina Jorre de St Jorre. Routledge, 2022: 30–40.

Jeannis, Hervens, James Joseph, Mary Goldberg, Katherine Seelman, Mark Schmeler, and Rory A. Cooper. "Full-Participation of Students with Physical Disabilities in Science and Engineering Laboratories." *Disability and Rehabilitation: Assistive Technology* 13, no. 2 (2018): 186–93.

Kapp, Steven. "How Social Deficit Models Exacerbate the Medical Model: Autism as Case in Point." *Autism Policy & Practice* 2, no. 1 (2019): 3–28.

———. *Autistic Community and the Neurodiversity Movement: Stories from the Frontline.* Palgrave Macmillan, 2020.

———. "Introduction." In *Autistic Community and the Neurodiversity Movement: Stories from the Frontline*, edited by Steven K. Kapp. Palgrave Macmillan, 2020: 1–19.

———. "Profound Concerns about 'Profound Autism': Dangers of Severity Scales and Functioning Labels for Support Needs." *Education Sciences* 13, no. 2 (2023): 106.

Katz, Jennifer. *Teaching to Diversity: The Three-Block Model of Universal Design for Learning*. Portage & Main Press, 2012.

Kezar, Adrianna, Tom DePaola, and Daniel T. Scott. *The Gig Academy: Mapping Labor in the Neoliberal University*. Johns Hopkins University Press, 2019.

King-Sears, Margaret. "Universal Design for Learning: Technology and Pedagogy." *Learning Disability Quarterly* 32, no. 4 (2009): 199–201.

Kober, Nancy. *Reaching Students: What Research Says about Effective Instruction in Undergraduate Science and Engineering*. National Academies Press, 2015.

Kohn, Alfie, and Susan D. Blum. *Ungrading: Why Rating Students Undermines Learning (and What to Do Instead)*. West Virginia University Press, 2020.

Konrad, Annika M. "Access Fatigue: The Rhetorical Work of Disability in Everyday Life." *College English* 83, no. 3 (2021): 179–99.

Kras, Joseph F. "The 'Ransom Notes' Affair: When the Neurodiversity Movement Came of Age." *Disability Studies Quarterly* 30, no. 1 (2010).

Kryger, Kathleen, and Griffin X. Zimmerman. "Neurodivergence and Intersectionality in Labor-Based Grading Contracts." *Journal of Writing Assessment* 13, no. 2 (2020).

Kuder, S. Jay, Amy Accardo, and John Woodruff. *College Success for Students on the Autism Spectrum: A Neurodiversity Perspective*. Taylor & Francis, 2023.

Ladau, Emily. "Why Person-First Language Doesn't Always Put the Person First," Maryland Coalition for Inclusive Education, 2015. https://mcie.org/think-inclusive/why-person-first-language-doesnt-always-put-the-person-first/.

Levinovitz, Alan. "Do Colleges Provide Too Many Disability Accommodations?" *Chronicle of Higher Education*, September 25, 2024. https://www.chronicle.com/article/do-colleges-provide-too-many-disability-accommodations?sra=true.

Lierman, Ash. *The Struggle You Can't See: Experiences of Neurodivergent and Invisibly Disabled Students in Higher Education*. Open Book Publishers, 2024.

Luterman, Sara. "Jordyn Zimmerman Is Redefining Communication as a Nonspeaking Advocate for Disability Rights." *The 19th*,

April 19, 2023. https://19thnews.org/2023/04/jordyn-zimmerman-nonspeaking-Autistic-advocate-communication/.

Marinus, Eva, Michelle Mostard, Eliane Segers, Teresa M. Schubert, Alison Madelaine, and Kevin Wheldall. "A Special Font for People with Dyslexia: Does It Work and, If So, Why?" *Dyslexia* 22, no. 3 (2016): 233–44.

Marist University, "Accommodations and Accessibility: Learning Support Program," n.d. https://www.marist.edu/student-life/community/accommodations-accessibility/learning-support.

McCreary, Michael. "Beyond Backward Design, or, by the End of This Article, You Should Be Able to Imagine Some Alternatives to Learning Objectives." *To Improve the Academy: A Journal of Educational Development* 41, no. 1 (2022): 68–91.

McKeon, Barbara, Carol S. Alpern, and Dianne Zager. "Promoting Academic Engagement for College Students with Autism Spectrum Disorder." *Journal of Postsecondary Education and Disability* 26, no. 4 (2013): 353–66.

McNeney, Arley (@Arley_McNeney). "I've been thinking about how access friction impacts my course design," Twitter (now X), March 6, 2022, https://x.com/Arley_McNeney/status/1500609017407688706?s=20.

Meyer, Anne, David H. Rose, and David Gordon. *Universal Design for Learning: Theory and Practice.* CAST Publishing, 2014.

Milton, Damian E. M. "On the Ontological Status of Autism: The 'Double Empathy Problem.'" *Disability & Society* 27, no. 6 (2012): 883–87.

Nachman, Brett Ranon. "'The Beacon on Campus': How an Autism-Specific Community College Support Program Addresses Ableism and Autism Acceptance." *College Student Affairs Journal* 41, no. 1 (2023): 31–45.

Ne'eman, Ari, and Elizabeth Pellicano. "Neurodiversity as Politics." *Human Development* 66, no. 2 (2022): 149–57.

Nzinga, Sekile M. *Lean Semesters: How Higher Education Reproduces Inequity.* JHU Press, 2020.

Olsen, Sara H., Stephanie Cork, Petra Anders, Ron Padrón, Alexandra Peterson, Amanda Strausser, and Paul T. Jaeger. "The Disability Tax and the Accessibility Tax: The Extra Intellectual, Emotional, and Technological Labor and Financial Expenditures Required of Disabled People in a World Gone Wrong . . . and Mostly Online." *Including Disability* 1 (2022): 51–86.

Oslund, Christy. *Supporting College and University Students with Invisible Disabilities: A Guide for Faculty and Staff Working with Students with*

Autism, AD/HD, Language Processing Disorders, Anxiety, and Mental Illness. Jessica Kingsley Publishers, 2013.

Pace, Kerry. "My Personal Experiences of Dyspraxia: Management Strategies and Resources for All." *AHEADjournal* 2 (2015). https://ahead.ie/journal/My-Personal-Experiences-of-Dyspraxia-Management-strategies-and-resources-for-all.

Parish, Peggy. *Thank You, Amelia Bedelia.* Illustrated by Fritz Siebel. Harper & Row, 1964.

Pitts Donahoe, Emily. "What Is Ungrading? What Is Collaborative Grading?" *Unmaking the Grade* (blog), January 3, 2025. https://emilypittsdonahoe.substack.com/p/what-is-ungrading-what-is-collaborative.

Poon, OiYan A., and Michael N. Bastedo. *Rethinking College Admissions: Research-Based Practice and Policy.* Harvard Education Press, 2022.

Pope-Ruark, Rebecca, Lee Skallerup Bessette, and Katie Rose Guest Pryal. *Of Many Minds: Neurodiversity and Mental Health Among University Faculty and Staff.* Johns Hopkins University Press, 2025.

Posselt, Julie R. *Inside Graduate Admissions: Merit, Diversity, and Faculty Gatekeeping.* Harvard University Press, 2016.

Price, Margaret. *Mad at School: Rhetorics of Mental Disability and Academic Life.* University of Michigan Press, 2011.

———. *Crip Spacetime: Access, Failure, and Accountability in Academic Life.* Duke University Press, 2024.

Pryal, Katie Rose Guest. "How to Teach Your (Many) Neurodivergent Students." *Chronicle of Higher Education,* March 29, 2023. https://www.chronicle.com/article/how-to-teach-your-many-neurodivergent-students.

———. *A Light in the Tower: A New Reckoning with Mental Health in Higher Education.* University Press of Kansas, 2024.

———. "Should You Seek an Adult Diagnosis of Neurodivergence?" *Chronicle of Higher Education,* January 22, 2024. https://www.chronicle.com/article/should-you-seek-an-adult-diagnosis-of-neurodivergence.

Rao, Kavita. "Inclusive Instructional Design: Applying UDL to Online Learning." *Journal of Applied Instructional Design* 10, no. 1 (2021): 83–97.

———, Jenna W. Gravel, David H. Rose, and T. Nicole Tucker-Smith. "Universal Design for Learning in Its 3rd Decade: A Focus on Equity, Inclusion, and Design." In *International Encyclopedia of Education,* 4th ed., edited by Robert J. Tierney, Fazal Rizvi, and Kadriye Ercikan. Elsevier Science, 2023: 712–20.

Reeves, Lillian. "Towards a Neuroinclusive Campus." Center for Academic Innovation & Faculty Support, University of South Carolina Upstate, May 9, 2024. https://web.archive.org/web/20250116180926/https:/blogs.uscupstate.edu/tip/2024/05/09/toward-a-neuroinclusive-campus/.

Regan, Ruti. "Social Skill: Theory of Mind," *Real Social Skills* (blog), September 4, 2012. https://realsocialskills.org/2012/09/04/social-skill-theory-of-mind/.

———. "Social Skill: Interacting with a Person Walking a Dog." *Real Social Skills* (blog), September 25, 2012. https://realsocialskills.org/2012/09/25/social-skill-interacting-with-a-person-walking-a-2/.

———. "Some Useful Phrases." *Real Social Skills* (blog), November 1, 2012. https://realsocialskills.org/2012/11/01/some-useful-phrases/.

———. "'Read the Syllabus': Getting the Information You Need without Annoying Your Instructors." *Real Social Skills* (blog), January 3, 2022. https://realsocialskills.org/2022/01/03/read-the-syllabus-getting-the-information-you-need-without-annoying-your-instructors/.

Rios, Jocelyn. "Positioned as a Burden: Analyzing the Participation of Multilingual Students of Color in Undergraduate Mathematics Courses that Use Groupwork." *Journal of Mathematical Behavior* 74 (2024): 101148.

Rodriguez, Marisella, and Sarah Silverman. "Horizontal Mentoring." In *Higher Education Careers Beyond the Professoriate,* edited by Karen Cardozo, Katherine Kearns, and Shannan Palma. Purdue University Press, 2024: 249–59.

Rose, David H., and Anne Meyer. *Teaching Every Student in the Digital Age: Universal Design for Learning.* ERIC, 2002.

Salvatore, Sophia, Claudia White, and Stephen Podowitz-Thomas. "'Not a Cookie Cutter Situation': How Neurodivergent Students Experience Group Work in Their STEM Courses." *International Journal of STEM Education* 11 (2024): 47.

Sander, Libby. "Seeking a Deft Touch for Students with Autism-Spectrum Disorders." *Chronicle of Higher Education,* June 2, 2013. https://www.chronicle.com/article/seeking-a-deft-touch-for-students-with-autism-spectrum-disorders/.

Schaefer, Jill, and Autumn Sanchez. "Shining a Light on Neurodiversity in Higher Ed," March 15, 2024. https://education.wisc.edu/news/shining-a-light-on-neurodiversity-in-higher-ed/.

Selingo, Jeffrey. *Who Gets In and Why: A Year Inside College Admissions.* Simon and Schuster, 2020.

Shakespeare, Tom. "The Social Model of Disability." In *The Disability Studies Reader*, 2nd ed., edited by Lennard J. Davis. Routledge, 2006: 16–24.

Silberman, Steve. *Neurotribes: The Legacy of Autism and the Future of Neurodiversity*. Penguin, 2015.

Sinclair, Jim. Don't Mourn for Us. Autistic Rights Movement UK, 1999.

———. "Autism Network International: The Development of a Community and its Culture." Autism Network International, January 2005, https://www.autreat.com/History_of_ANI.html.

Singer, Judy "Why Can't You Be Normal for Once in Your Life?: From a 'Problem with No Name' to a New Category of Disability." In *Disability Discourse*, edited by Mairian Corker and Sally French. McGraw-Hill, 1999: 59–67.

Smagorinsky, Peter. "Neurodiversity and the Deep Structure of Schools." *Ought: The Journal of Autistic Culture* 2, no. 1 (2020): 10–35.

Smith, Laura. "'I Am a Minimally Speaking Autistic Person Who Was Not Expected to Go to College.' Now He's Getting His PhD." *California*, March 21, 2021. https://alumni.berkeley.edu/california-magazine/2022-fall/i-am-a-minimally-speaking-person-who-was-not-expected-to-go-to-college-now-hes-getting-his-phd/.

Snyder, Sharon, and David Mitchell. "Afterword—Regulated Bodies: Disability Studies and the Controlling Professions." In *Social Histories of Disability and Deformity*, edited by David M. Turner and Kevin Stagg. Routledge, 2006: 175–89.

Taboas, Amanda, Karla Doepke, and Corinne Zimmerman. "Preferences for Identity-First versus Person-First Language in a US Sample of Autism Stakeholders." *Autism* 27, no. 2 (2023): 565–70.

Tinker, Sarah C., Rebecca H. Bitsko, Melissa L. Danielson, Kimberly Newsome, and Jennifer W. Kaminski. "Estimating the Number of People with Tourette Syndrome and Persistent Tic Disorder in the United States." *Psychiatry Research* 314 (2022): 114684.

Tisoncik, Laura A. "Autistics.Org and Finding Our Voices as an Activist Movement." In *Autistic Community and the Neurodiversity Movement: Stories from the Frontline*, edited by Steven K. Kapp. Palgrave Macmillan, 2020: 65–76.

Tucker, Richard, and Neda Abbasi. "Bad Attitudes: Why Design Students Dislike Teamwork." *Journal of Learning Design* 9, no. 1 (2016): 1–20.

Vidali, Amy. "Texts of Our Institutional Lives: Performing the Rhetorical Freak Show: Disability, Student Writing, and College Admissions." *College English* 69, no. 6 (2007): 615–41.

Walker, Nick. *Neuroqueer Heresies: Notes on the Neurodiversity Paradigm, Autistic Empowerment, and Postnormal Possibilities.* Autonomous Press, 2021.

Wei, Xin, Elizabeth R. A. Christiano, Jennifer W. Yu, Jose Blackorby, Paul Shattuck, and Lynn A. Newman. "Postsecondary Pathways and Persistence for STEM versus Non-STEM Majors: Among College Students with an Autism Spectrum Disorder." *Journal of Autism and Developmental Disorders* 44, no. 5 (2014): 1159–67.

Wells, Joe. "I Am Autistic," comedy special, 2023, posted October 27, 2023, by Joe Wells, YouTube. https://www.youtube.com/watch?v=JCcH2jZVFtk.

Wendell, Susan. *The Rejected Body: Feminist Philosophical Reflections on Disability.* Routledge, 1996.

Williamson, Bess. *Accessible America: A History of Disability and Design.* New York University Press, 2019.

Winkelmes, Mary-Ann, Allison Boye, and Suzanne Tapp. *Transparent Design in Higher Education Teaching and Leadership: A Guide to Implementing the Transparency Framework Institution-Wide to Improve Learning and Retention.* Taylor & Francis, 2023.

Wise, Sonny Jane. *We're All Neurodiverse: How to Build a Neurodiversity-Affirming Future and Challenge Neuronormativity.* Jessica Kingsley Publishers, 2023.

Zaloom, Caitlin. *Indebted: How Families Make College Work at Any Cost.* Princeton University Press, 2019.

INDEX

Note: Page numbers with the letter "n" indicate endnotes.

TEACHING, ENGAGING, AND THRIVING IN HIGHER ED SERIES

James M. Lang and Michelle D. Miller,
Series Editors

Other books in the series:

A Pedagogy of Kindness
Catherine J. Denial

A Teacher's Guide to Learning Student Names:
Why You Should, Why It's Hard, How You Can
Michelle D. Miller

The Present Professor:
Authenticity and Transformational Teaching
Elizabeth A. Norell

The Opposite of Cheating:
Teaching for Integrity in the Age of AI
Tricia Bertram Gallant and David A. Rettinger

Making Writing Meaningful:
A Guide for Higher Education
Michele Eodice, Anne Ellen Geller, and Neal Lerner

Snafu EDU:
Teaching and Learning When Things Go Wrong in the College Classroom
Jessamyn Neuhaus

Empowered:
A Woman Faculty of Color's Guide to Teaching and Thriving
Chavella T. Pittman

The Joyful Online Teacher:
Finding Our Fizz in Asynchronous Classes
Flower Darby

UDL at Scale:
Whole-Campus Universal Design for Learning
Thomas J. Tobin

www.ingramcontent.com/pod-product-compliance
Lightning Source LLC
LaVergne TN
LVHW101626040926
847296LV00026B/113

* 9 7 8 0 8 0 6 1 9 7 2 0 3 *